MW00768016

Caught Up In God's Presence

Are We going to be Left Behind?

Jaemin H. Park

and

Josh Stewart

Protea Publihsing
ATLANTA

website: www.covenant-study.com

All scripture quotations are taken from NIV unless otherwise
noted.

Published by:
Protea Publishing Company
Atlanta, Georgia, USA

email: kaolink@msn.com

website: www.proteapublishing.com

ISBN 1-883707-33-1

**Dedicated to Charlie Stewart
for his sincere support.**

To the whiter,
lots of blessings
to your family

Jasmin U. Park

Prologue: Luther's refusal

For nearly fifteen centuries from the time of Jesus Christ, Western Christianity was predominated by the Catholic Church, which reigned over Europe and influenced it both spiritually and politically. As the church implemented itself more to political affairs than the religious one, the institution slowly decayed. By 1500s, a pontiff was no different from a local prince. Especially, after the reigns of Alexander VI and Julius II, the papacy had become a mere principality. The institution itself was corrupted; nepotism and bribery thrived. The church deviated so drastically from its first century counterpart that the 16th century Catholic Church was inappropriate to call itself the dwelling place for God.[1]

It was the Reformation that kindled countless souls to reform the Catholic Church that contradicted its doctrine with the reality.[2] This Reformation movement spread throughout Europe during the 16th century and finally resulted in the Thirty Years War in Europe. Its impact was so immense that it completely turned the world upside down. After the war, Catholicism gradually declined while the Protestant denominations reigned supreme over Northern Europe, and later North America. In fact, most contemporary Christian denominations originate from this movement.

The Reformation is not a single event but rather series of events, however, they all began with Luther's refusal to submit to the church which had the tradition of thousand years behind it. One college history book gives a detailed account for this incident.

Unable to accept Luther's forcefully worded dissent from traditional Catholic teachings, the church excommunicated him in January 1521. He was also summoned to appear before the imperial diet or Reichstag of the Holy Roman Empire, convened by the newly elected emperor Charles V. Expected to recant the heretical doctrines he had espoused, Luther refused and made the famous reply that became the battle cry of the Reformation, "Since then

Your Majesty and your lordships desire a simple reply, I will answer without horns and without teeth. Unless I am convicted by Scripture and plain reason — I do not accept the authority of popes and councils, for they have contradicted each other — my conscience is captive to the Word of God. I cannot and I will not recant anything, for to go against conscience is neither right nor safe. Here I stand, I cannot do otherwise. God help me. Amen."[3]

The young emperor Charles was outraged of Luther's audacity and gave his opinion that "A SINGLE FRIAR WHO GOES COUNTER TO ALL CHRISTIANITY FOR A THOUSAND YEARS MUST BE WRONG."[4]

⌘

Introduction: truth vs. tradition

"You have let go of the commands of God and are holding on to the traditions of men,"[5] is what Jesus said to the Pharisees when they accused his disciples of being disobedient to the tradition of the elders. This short, yet concise, phrase depicts not only the attitude of the Pharisees but as well as us, contemporary Christians. Nearly two millennia have passed from the time of Jesus Christ, how much progress did we make from those Pharisees who worshipped tradition over the truth? Are we not repeating same mistakes again? It is difficult to admit, but our two thousand years history from the time of Christ consisted of conflicts between the truth and tradition.

We read about the Pharisees and say, "If I was living back then, then I would not have made such an obvious mistake as crucifying the Son of God." But we should also realize, that those Pharisees had the exact, same attitude as we do now in 20th century. They said, "If we had lived in the days of our ancestors, we would not have taken part with them in shedding the blood of the prophets."[6] Just look at what they did, these same people, who made such a confident statement, took part in killing of the Lord, Jesus Christ!

There is an absolute difference between knowing history and applying the knowledge learned from history. History repeats itself, and by studying in historical context, we learn how to deal with situations that our ancestors dealt with. The same principal applies while reading the Bible. Remember that the Bible is a 1st century book, not a 20th century product. We, the students of the Word, should know more than anyone else that the Bible, and it should be read from the 1st century perspective rather than our modern, post-industrial one.

I am attempting to restore us, Christians, the original inspiration that our 1st century counterparts possessed. Contemporary Christian doctrine is not as solid as it used to be, and our world is experiencing a dramatic moral decline. The decline is partially due to the fact that the contemporary Christianity did not truthfully serve its role as the holy temple of the

Lord.[7] Our doctrine is filled with unbiblical traditional concepts; unfortunately, these traditional perceptions dwell in our hearts as well.

Studying the eschatology in historical context is the only way to attain the original 1st century inspiration. Our contemporary expectation of being caught up in the air must be replaced with the 1st century classical concept of being caught up in God's presence. Living in God's presence is what the humanity has longed for since its creation.

It is my strong conviction to reform the church; by clarifying the eschatological - theological issues we will eliminate our denominational boundaries and gather every Christian under one building, the temple of the Lord. For the temple of the Lord is not a building made by human hands, instead, it is made by God's hands. The church of third millennium must eliminate denominational boundaries in order to become a lamp stand of the third millennium.

Our search for the truth may be interrupted with traditional bias. However, as long as the truth is still attainable, then you will eventually reach its destination. Do not worry about getting lost because the Lord is our shepherd, and he is the one who is leading the way. Explore the Bible as much as you desire; the truth is nearer than where you would expect it to be.

⌘

Acknowledgements

Making of Caught Up in God's Presence wouldn't have been possible without Charlie, who provided consistent support for publishing the book, and Jesse, without whom I wouldn't have had an opportunity to study eschatology. On January 17th of 2000, with an invitation from Jesse, I attended Doug King's Bible study without a slight expectation of how much influence I would receive due to this course of action.

I should give credit to Doug for being an excellent teacher. He has been a guide in my quest for the truth. I should thank Doug's wife Denee, and her mom Elaine as well for the constant support.

Charlie's wife, Anita should receive some attention for her assistance in this publication. John Byerley, who was a committed audience of the book's drafts, should be acknowledged as well.

Attending Atlanta Millennial Forum in February 2000 and Transmillennial™ Conference in June 2000 granted me chances to meet with several eminent leaders of transmillennial™ movement, including Jay Gary, Tim King, and Max R. King. Without them, the movement itself would not have existed.

I'd like to express my gratitude to Johan Du Toit who runs the Protea Publishing Company for his support in this publication. There are many unnamed people that I should acknowledge for their indirect participation in making of Caught Up in God's Presence, including some teachers and friends in my school. They had been the motivation that kept me enthusiastic and committed in my spiritual quest. Finally, I would like to thank God, for all the wonderful works He has done for us.

⌘

Table Of Contents

5. The Arrival of Christ

6. Neo-Reformation

Epilogue: Reforming the church through eschatology

⌘

1. Essentials in Christian Eschatology

1.1. The True Open Mind

Some people will say that they will listen with an open mind, but when they actually sit down and study the scripture, there are notions of the exact opposite. The problem is that they are lying to themselves because they do not want to picture themselves as a closed-minded person. A change needs to begin when they discover the truth of how they look at scripture. If they just ignore the possibility, then they are already depriving themselves a chance to find out the truth.

Looking at things with a true, open mind will assist the situation, and it will not cause any unethical disputes among Christians. One of the main reasons that people have trouble looking at things with an open mind is because they let their emotions get in the way of studying the Bible. Emotions are not bad or unusual, but they can cause an immense distraction while trying to study scripture. The mind will not listen while the heart is screaming. This is why I ask you to relax your heart and give your mind an opportunity to validly listen to all that is written.

If Christians know that they are being told about a different view, then they should, temporarily, put aside all of their own beliefs and deep convictions. When the view is presented, the view of the listener may have a disagreement during presentation, and there will be a spiritual conflict within the mind of the listener. In most cases, a rejection will occur to everything that was or is to be said during the presentation. As it is easy to see, this conflict will have the offspring of a closed-mind. The only way to make sure that there is no conflict between both views is to have the listener put away their own beliefs for a period of time. This challenge may seem difficult to accomplish, but it is a requirement in order to achieve a true, open mind. Also, keep in mind: this is all for the benefit of the listener so that they can seek the truth without having to deal with a closed mind.

After the presentation, evaluate the elements presented in comparison to one's own view and make changes where the believer truly feels that it is necessary. If this step is omitted, then the reading of the presentation was in vain, and the challenges made in the presentation will not set into place. Also, not making the changes in one's view will cause excessive confidence, and change will become harder to make in other situations. This type of confidence is not a characteristic of God; as a Christian, this is the type of emotional behavior that should not occur because we are called to be humble in our studies, not boastful. If we boast in our studies, then one's intentions are not focused on God. These are conceded intentions that are against the benefit of the truth.

The overall consequence of lacking an open mind: even if there is any truth in the opposing belief, then it is automatically rejected by their emotions. Seeking the truth is the reason for all study, and if we take away the truth, then there is no reason to believe in God because he is the absolute truth. Trying to find the truth should be motivating enough for everyone to put aside their emotion and give an honest look at another person's view. The truth is what will set us free from all mystery, speculation, and tradition.

⌘

1.2. Enslaved to the Physical Realm

What is the importance of physical existence? Do you exist so that you are able to receive the temporary, minor elements of physical life (i.e. satisfaction, emotions, materialistic items, etc.)? Naturally, these are some of things that we like about life, but is that what God has in purpose for our lives? God is everlasting and the relationship that we have with him is eternal. In our lives, should we emphasize the physical or the spiritual? It is very hard to make this change of mindset since nature persists on the physical. Let us take a look at a passage from Romans because it contrasts the physical and the spiritual: "Those who live according to the sinful nature have their minds set on what that nature desires; but those who live in accordance with the Spirit have their minds set on what the Spirit desires. The mind of sinful man is death, but the mind controlled by the Spirit is life and peace; the sinful mind is hostile to God. It does not submit to God's law, nor can it do so."[8] As you can see, it extremely opposes God's nature to live for these physical elements, and we are called to adjust our outlook.

Ever since my physical existence, my spirit coexisted, but the origin of my spiritual existence is unknown. I had received my spiritual life (not existence, there is a difference) when I was saved from my slavery of sin[9] at the proclamation of my faith or baptism[10] whichever you believe. That was the time that I received spiritual, everlasting life, and life is an inheritance[11] from God that no one can take away from me.

What happens to our existence after our physical life expires? When the physical aspects of your life perish, what happens next? Once you have experienced the physical filter (or physical death), then there will never be a time when your mind malfunctions. You may not be able to see, touch, smell, hear, or taste but you will always be able to think. These are the things that I am certain in my convictions, and these events will occur after physical death. Logically, if we do no longer exist physically, then many physical elements (i.e. satisfaction, emotions, materialistic items, etc.) will cease to exist when our physical body perishes. The idea of non-physical existence may seem hard to comprehend, but this is the challenge that is being made in hope to change one's mindset. One thing to always remember: your physical existence is temporary, and there will be a day when we must rely on our spiritual existence. After obtaining this knowledge, you must begin to realize that you might as well begin to think on spiritual terms for the benefit of your intentions and your actions.

In a letter to the Corinthians, Paul writes this about our physical and spiritual existence: "If there is a natural body, there is also a spiritual body."[12] This statement is highly valid, but does Paul say the opposite (If there is a spiritual body, there is also a natural body) is true? No, he does not because the physical is only a mere shadow of the greater, everlasting spiritual[13] things to come. If we were still in our physical bodies, then when would be the point of time in which the spiritual things would be established? After physical death is the time in which all physical things cease, this is also the time in which all spiritual things become independent. Recognize this about that passage: it does tell about a time in which the physical and the spiritual coexist. While this time period is occurring, there are conflicts of the physical and the spiritual because they are coexisting, and I believe this time period is after baptism or proclamation of faith but before physical death.

Can it be possible that we are no longer in bondage to sin, but still enslaved to the physical realm? I have seen people that claim to be Christians who are still enslaved to the physical realm, but I cannot be the one to say that their sins are forgiven. This question is one to think about on a personal level, and I do not want to come to any conclusions on this specific issue. Please consider all evidences that have been presented and deeply think about this topic. I would like to leave you with this last statement (in order to make an impact within your own life): how much greater is a spiritual change than a physical change?

⌘

1.3. The Context of Scripture

Was the Bible written for the sake of a 20th Century reader? This answer is simple; but yet, it is so hard for some people to understand. If I decided to write you a letter, do you think that my letter, which contains highly specific details about you, should be applied to a different group of people 2,000 years later? As you can see, the obvious answer is "no", but why do people hold the Bible to be an exception from such logic? It may be because of tradition, or it may be because they do not understand the historical context of scripture. Either way, the problem with looking at the Bible in a 20th Century perspective is that the Epistles in the New Testament were actual letters that were received by a specific audience, not 20th Century Christians.

Do I believe that the audience understood almost every detail of these letters? Yes, otherwise, there would have been no point in writing the letter, correct? Even most prophecies made sense to the audience that received them, because it was written in the apocalyptic code that most Jews of that time were familiar with. Since most Christians, today, never read the Old Testament or do not understand it, then this code has lost the original meaning of the 1st Century Christians. This issue may be a larger problem than it seems at first; I'm assured that this problem will arise again.

What are the consequences of misinterpretation of scripture? Generally, it will cause contradictions related to other passages in the Bible, and it can cause a false outlook of Christ. Interpreting scripture requires much more than just a literal interpretation because if you are not involved with it, then it is very difficult to fit all of the pieces together. One of the hardest things to decide is the question, "What statements still apply to today?" Although we are not living in the 1st Century, I believe that many principles still apply, but I would not make any applications about signs or warnings because many of these things were not written to us. As a 20th Century Christian, it becomes more complicated dealing with the signs because most of us has not established our 'status' today. If we do not know what our 'status' is, then how can we decide which scriptures apply today? Some people simply state that all scripture applies today, because they believe that the Bible was written directly to them. However, once we discover our 'status', then we might see why historical context is a significant factor.

Validity and inspiration of God are only two of the most important elements in Christianity. Paul writes in a letter to Timothy: "All Scripture is God-breathed and is useful for teaching, rebuking, correcting and training in righteousness, so that the man of God may be thoroughly equipped for every good work."[14] This proves the practical use for scripture, and God inspired all of the scripture, not just the ones about Christ as the Messiah. Some people truly believe that some statements made in the Bible are distorted, but this is an obvious excuse for just rejecting the scripture that they do not want to hear. This verse is not taking away the importance of the historical context of the letters because it just describes the inspiration and use of scripture. The historical context of the Bible must be let in while presuppositions of the reader should be left out. Presuppositions are not universal, unlike the Bible, but they will always remain a persistent factor while trying to study scripture.

⌘

1.4. Prophetic Language

Please note this passage before reading this chapter. "And we have the word of the prophets made more certain, and you will do well to pay attention to it, as to a light shining in a dark place, until the day dawns and the morning star rises in your hearts. Above all, you must understand that no prophecy of Scripture came about by the prophet's own interpretation. For prophecy never had its origin in the will of man, but men spoke from God as they were carried along by the Holy Spirit."[15]

What is prophetic language? It is literally a type of language used to record the prophecies given through prophets by the Holy Spirit. The prophetic language contains many symbolism and imageries, which makes it difficult for a student of the Word to interpret the prophecies.

Wail, for the day of the Lord is near;
it will come like destruction from the Almighty!
Because of this, all hands will go limp,
Every man's heart will melt.
Terror will seize them, pain and anguish will grip them;
they will writhe like a woman in labor.
They will look aghast at each other,
their faces aflame.

See, the day of the Lord is coming,
a cruel day, with wrath and fierce anger,
To make the land desolate
and destroy the sinners within it.
The stars of heaven and their constellations
will not show their light.
The rising sun will be darkened
and the moon will not give its light.[16]

My Bible commentary states that this prophecy had been fulfilled after two centuries from the time Isaiah died.[17] I'm not going to argue whether their interpretation is correct or not. The point is that the commentators admit that this prophecy was to be written in symbolic language. Here's an identical prophecy from the gospel of Matthew:

> *Immediately after the distress of those days*
> *'the sun will be darkened,*
>   *and the moon will not give its light;*
> *the starts will fall from the sky,*
>   *and the heavenly bodies will be shaken.'*[18]

Does this prophecy sound symbolic to you? I'm certain that everybody would admit so. However, look up the verse after this verse (v.29). What does it say?

> *At that time the sign of the Son of Man will appear in the sky, and all the nations of the earth will mourn. They will see the Son of Man coming on the clouds of the sky, with power and great glory. And he will send his angels with a loud trumpet call, and they will gather his elect from the four winds, from one end of the heavens to the other.*[19]

What is your attitude toward this particular passage? Does it still sound symbolic, or should this passage be interpreted literally? I pointed out already that this language was actually used first in the prophecy of Isaiah. My point is that the innumerable New Testament prophecies are actually the recitals of the Old Testament prophecies. The style of language used in the particular passage above depicted that Jesus actually used Isaiah's symbolism to prophesy about the day of the Lord.

Let us examine some words from the above passage that I cited. Note the word "trumpet". This trumpet has crucial significance on the Day of the Lord. They are mentioned throughout the whole Bible, but we Christians are more familiar with those words being used in the New Testament prophecies. Here are some passages from the New Testament where the word "trumpet" is used:

The Old Testament is in abundance of these symbolic languages. If we interpret the Old Testament prophecies too literally, we end up spoiling the true meaning of the prophecies. Here's an example of the Old Testament prophecy – by

Isaiah - concerning the doom of Babylon.

Note the imageries and symbols contained in the passage:

Listen, I tell you a mystery: We will not all sleep, but we will all be changed – in a flash, in the twinkling of an eye, at the last TRUMPET. For the TRUMPET will sound, the dead will be raised imperishable, and we will be changed. For the perishable must clothe itself with the imperishable, and the mortal with immortality.[20]

From this verse, we discover that the trumpet triggers the resurrection of the dead, as it said "the dead will be raised imperishable, and we will be changed." This is the significance of the trumpet, let's look at other books to see how the word "trumpet" is used.

According to the Lord's own word, we tell you that we who are still alive, who are left till the coming of the Lord, will certainly not precede those who have fallen asleep. For the Lord himself will come down from heaven, with a loud command, with the voice of the archangel and with the TRUMPET call of God, and the dead in Christ will rise first. After that, we who are still alive and are left will be caught up together with them in the clouds to meet the Lord in the air. And so we will be with the Lord forever.[21]

Now it is clear that this trumpet is the beginning sign for the resurrection of the dead. It doesn't necessary have to be the literal trumpet sounding, the thing that matters is the significance of the trumpet. Is there any Old Testament passage that mentions the trumpet? Where did the trumpet originate?

The Lord said to Moses: "Make two trumpets of hammered silver, and use them for calling the community together and for having the camps set out. When both are sounded, the whole community is to assemble before you at the entrance to the Tent of Meeting. If only one is sounded, the leaders – the heads of the clans of Israel – are to assemble before you. When a trumpet blast is sounded, the tribes camping on the east are to set out. At the sounding of a second blast, the camps on the south are to set out. The blast will signal for the setting out. To gather the assembly, blow the trumpets, but not with the same signal.

"The sons of Aaron, the priests, are to blow the trumpets. This is to be a lasting ordinance for you and the generations to come. When you go into battle in your own land against an enemy who is oppressing you, sound a blast on the trumpets. Then you will be remembered by the LORD your God and rescued from your enemies. Also at your times of rejoicing – your appointed feasts and New Moon festivals – you are to sound the trumpets over your burnt offerings and fellowship offerings, and they will be a memorial for you before your God. I am the LORD your God."[22]

These verses from Numbers show that the trumpet called and directed people. When our New Testament says, "For the Lord himself will descend from heaven with… the trumpet of God," we should see this as symbolic of a gathering. God never meant for literalism to spoil the spiritual meaning.

Clouds[23] speak of God's power and presence at work to affect a particular task; in our passage it is the resurrection. Air, in Biblical language, speaks of a spiritual environment populated by personalities without fleshly bodies. We could go on, but surely the reader appreciates that the rich language of symbolism conveys much truth with few words. But consider this: How much do we lose when we insist upon bringing literal interpretation to symbolic imagery?[24]

⌘

1.5. Seeking the Spiritual Quest.

Above chapters dealt with basic, yet essentials in understanding the Word of God. The Bible can be interpreted
in million different ways. Everybody lives with his/her own
interpretation of the things, and the Bible is no exception. It
is important to realize God tries to communicate with you
through the Bible. In order to comprehend God's message, we
should understand what the Bible is all about.

There's a single theme for which the Bible exists, the
issue of sin and death, and how God deals with that issue to
bring His children toward salvation. The sin and death was
brought through Adam, the first man. However, Jesus Christ
– the second Adam, has made perfect forever those who believe
in him. We have been made holy through the sacrifice of the
body of Jesus Christ once for all.[25] This is the general framework of the entire Bible.

A student of the Word also should acknowledge – before
studying the Bible, all the scripture is inspired by God. The
Bible was written by the divine inspiration called the Holy
Spirit. Without faith in all God's words, there is no point in
studying the Bible. Studying the Bible may bring us to a point
to choose whether to accept new hidden ideas or to retain our
old concepts. In that case, I suggest that you remind yourself
that the Bible is not written by mere men, but with God's
inspiration.

There are a considerable number of people who believe
that the Bible cannot be logically proven. I personally had con-
versations with some atheists; they strongly insist that the Bible
is full of contradictions. Here's another necessity for studying
the Word of God.[26] As Christians, we should be able to prove
the skeptics, that the Bible is the truth indeed. Luckily, there
are many fulfilled prophecies of the Bible that are proven both
logically and scientifically. For example, the fall of Jerusalem
(AD 70) was prophesied in the gospels of Matthew, Luke, and
Mark. There is no dispute over this argument, as a conse-

quence of this proof, many skeptics insist the Bible being written on the later date, near AD 90, or as far as AD 110.

Therefore, understanding the Bible to its fulness is essential in our spiritual walk with Christ. The Bible has a single unified theme. Here's a quote from a senior theologian, Max R. King. His words express my message better than anything else when preaching the oneness of the Bible:

In the search for Truth, and our quest for oneness in doctrine, understanding and practice, have we no choice but to settle for a façade of unity in the midst of a wild and restless sea of diversity? I do not think so. I believe there is remarkable unity and continuity of divine purpose in scripture, that this is not merely a dream or an illusion of man. The Bible can be read, understood, believed, and practiced if there is the heart and the will to do so.[27]

If there's a will, it can be done. The Bible doesn't necessary have to be so difficult. Searching the truth within the Bible takes some research, but it wouldn't be so difficult if there's a will. My fellow students of the Word, I'd like to inform you that from the moment you open the next chapter, you will begin a spiritual quest for the truth, which is going to last for your entire lifetime. In this journey you will confront many frustrations and obstacles, both physically and mentally. Pray that God will guide you the way in your spiritual quest for the truth. Ask, and it will be given to you; seek and you will find; knock and the door will be opened to you. For everyone who asks receives; he who seeks finds; and to him who knocks, the door will be opened.[28]

⌘

2. Covenantal Perspective

2.1. Problems with the Law

In this chapter, we will be analyzing the lives of people that were under the law. Although we are not under the law, we still need to understand the results of the law in order to be able to appreciate the grace. Many Christians want to omit the step of studying about the Old Covenant, but studying the Old Covenant is the best way to understand the New Covenant. As the inspired followers of Christ, we will look back upon the Old Covenant; then we will be able to see why Jesus died on the Cross.

Let us begin by reading 2 Corinthians 3:7-11, "Now if the ministry that brought death, which was engraved in letters on stone, came with glory, so that the Israelites could not look steadily at the face of Moses because of its glory, fading though it was, will not the ministry of the Spirit be even more glorious? If the ministry that condemns men is glorious, how much more glorious is the ministry that brings righteousness! For what was glorious has no glory now in comparison with the surpassing glory. And if what **was fading away**[29] came with glory, how much greater is the glory of that which lasts!" The first idea to recognize is that this passage is contrasting the Old and New Covenants; and secondly, the Ten Commandments were written on stone tablets. This passage emphasizes the Old Covenant's correlation to the physical realm because its laws were written on stone tablets unlike the New Covenant[30]. The Old Covenant emphasized the physical and brought death; the New Covenant gave life through the spirit. Both complete covenants would have no common ground, and this is why Peter's ministry took a period of time to fully convert the Judaizers (Jews that were still zealous of the law after the resurrection of Jesus).

Why does the scripture say that this ministry (Old Covenant) brought death? The reason is because sin separates us from God, and when sin is full-grown, then it gives birth to death[31]. Paul quotes the core problem of sin: "The sting of death is sin, and the power of sin is the law."[32] When analyzing this problem, there is no logical way that definition of death is physical, because the New Covenant is the exact opposite of the Old Covenant, correct? When I turn to John 3:16, it says, "…whoever believes in him shall not perish but have eternal life." If I believe in Jesus (this is what 'him' refers to in this verse), then will I obtain eternal physical life? Is this why Jesus died on the cross, so that I could exist physically forever? No! But, concerning the resurrection of the dead, this verse (John 3:16) will be frequently related because it says that the believer shall not perish. When the Bible talks about people that were clothed perishable[33], this has nothing to do with physical bodies because the New Covenant does not give eternal physical life.

As Romans 6:16 says, "Don't you know that when you offer yourselves to someone to obey him as slaves, you are slaves to the one whom you obey--whether you are slaves to sin, which leads to death, or to obedience, which leads to righteousness?" being enslaved to sin leads to death. If we are slaves to sin, then we are living under the Old Covenant. Today, there is a way out to be set free from our bondage of sin through Jesus Christ because he sets us free![34] The people that existed under the Old Covenant did not have this same message, and they did not have a way out of their slavery because Hebrews 10:1-4 affirms, "The law is only a shadow of the good things that are coming--not the realities themselves. For this reason it can never, by the same sacrifices repeated endlessly year after year, make perfect those who draw near to worship. If it could, would they not have stopped being offered? For the worshipers would have been cleansed once for all, and would no longer have felt guilty for their sins. But those sacrifices are an annual reminder of sins, because it is impossible for the blood of bulls and goats to take away sins." If these sacrifices did not take away sin, then what would happen to those that died before Jesus' atonement was complete? "Now we know that whatever the law says, it says to those who are under the law, so that every mouth may be silenced and the whole world held accountable to God."[35] They would be held accountable and judged by their works: "All who sin apart from the law will also perish apart from the law, and all who sin under the law will be judged by the law."[36] The judgment of accountability was to take place would be given to those under the law to determine if they were worthy of life brought through Jesus Christ.[37]

The law cursed everyone that lived under it because Galatians 3:10-14 state: "All who rely on observing the law are under a curse, for it is written: Cursed is everyone who does not continue to do everything written in the Book of the Law. Clearly no one is justified before God by the law, because, the righteous will live by faith. The law is not based on faith; on the contrary, the man who does these things will live by them. Christ redeemed us from the curse of the law by becoming a curse for us, for it is written: Cursed is everyone who is hung on a tree. He redeemed us in order that the blessing given to Abraham might come to the Gentiles through Christ Jesus, so that by faith we might receive the promise of the Spirit." Although the word 'curse' is an English translation, a curse was something brought upon them by a superior power as a result of doing things their own way, and they had no control of when this 'curse' would go away. Jesus is the one and had the timing that would bring them out of this 'curse' so they could acquire their promise of the spirit. When the Jews in the early church rejected Jesus, they did not only just reject his beliefs, but they rejected his fulfillment of the promise that would take them out of their bondage.

I hope that I have painted a crisp picture of the life of a premessianic (life before the Messiah) Jew. This is crucial when trying to understand the conflict of the first century. This covenantal perspective is the foundation of interpreting all scripture because the Bible opens with the problem of sin and closes with the resolution. Now that we have identified the problem, then the next chapter will follow through with the resolution. As you go along reading all of the chapters, let this 'problem and resolution' perspective flow so that you will be able to receive the answers to questions: 'why' and 'how' about the Bible.

⌘

2.2. Resolution to Sin

We have recognized the problem of sin, and we have read the verses about the effects of the law. In this chapter, I want to recognize the covenantal solution of sin's problem. In order to resolve this problem, God designed and placed a New Covenant that could allow his people to 'get around' this problem. God united himself with us because we are no longer dead to our sin. If we were dead, then we would be separated from God, but since God established a New Covenant, he has allowed us to dwell in his presence. We will be looking at how this process took place.

Faith was not always an option, and it did not just appear from nowhere. How was the slavery of sin abolished? "Therefore, there is now no condemnation for those who are in Christ Jesus, because through Christ Jesus the law of the Spirit of life set me free from the law of sin and death. For what the law was powerless to do in that it was weakened by the sinful nature, God did by sending his own Son in the likeness of sinful man to be a sin offering. And so he condemned sin in sinful man, in order that the righteous requirements of the law might be fully met in us, who do not live according to the sinful nature but according to the Spirit."[38] God sent his son as a sin offering for us, and he fulfilled the requirements of righteousness under the law. The Old Covenant was put into place, so that God could demonstrate that no one could achieve salvation by one's own ability, and when the time was right, God would send his son to abolish this dreadful law because it only brought spiritual death to his beloved people. Jesus' perfect observance of the law, sacrifice, resurrection, and atonement were all works of God, and no person could accomplish all of these things. God did all of these works to bring: the restoration of his presence, salvation, and fulfillment of all promises. Jesus' deeds were not for himself, but his works brought a new creation to everyone. These particular deeds enabled him to spread salvation to everyone, but he only asked for one simple request from us in return. He asked us to love and keep faith in him, and when we do so, we are guaranteed our salvation.

"For sin shall not be your master, because you are not under law, but under grace. What then? Shall we sin because we are not under law but under grace? By no means!"[39] We are under grace, but sin should not flow through us without even thinking. This is a very hard concept to learn and practice, but my interpretation of these verses may be useful. I think that this verse is saying that we are under the grace of God and have a secure salvation, but that does not mean that we should 'trash' our morals or give up trying on life. Salvation requires faith, and if I place my faith into something, then I will continue to do good deeds because I want to grow in my faith. A faith that does not desire to grow cannot realistically be considered a faith at all.

"The time is coming," declares the LORD, "when I will make a new covenant with the house of Israel and with the house of Judah. It will not be like the covenant I made with their forefathers when I took them by the hand to lead them out of Egypt, because they broke my covenant, though I was a husband to them, " declares the LORD. "This is the covenant I will make with the house of Israel after that time," declares the LORD. "I will put my law in their minds and write it on their hearts. I will be their God, and they will be my people. No longer will a man teach his neighbor, or a man his brother, saying, `Know the LORD,' because they will all know me, from the least of them to the greatest," declares the LORD. "For I will forgive their wickedness and will remember their sins no more."[40] Jeremiah spoke this prophecy in the Old Testament, and it was fulfilled at the unveiling of the New Covenant. Although this was a promise that was made directly to Israel, there were also promises made for the Gentiles so that they would receive the light of salvation.[41] Back to the central promise, the LORD said that in the New Covenant, he would not remember their sins and forgive transgression. This promise was not comfortable among the premessianic Jews, and they highly anticipated their total redemption from sin. Let us look at the fulfillment of this promise in the New Testament, "No one who is born of God will continue to sin, because God's seed remains in him; he cannot go on sinning, because he has been born of God."[42] Once we are born of God, we do not sin any longer. How is this possible? "For if those who live by law are heirs, faith has no value and the promise is worthless, because law brings wrath. And where there is no law, there is no transgression."[43] The context of this scripture is speaking about those that live by faith in Christ, and this does not apply to those that lack faith. When the verse talks about those born of God that do no sin, the interpretation of the verse should not be taken literally because every person still attempts to do things his/her own way, but God does not remember our sin because of the establishment of the New Covenant and the deportation of the Old Covenant. Otherwise, if this verse was saying that we do not sin literally, then it would be contradictory with this verse: "If we claim to be without sin, we deceive ourselves and the truth is not in us."[44]

"Seventy 'sevens' are decreed for your people and your holy city to finish transgression, to put an end to sin, to atone for wickedness, to bring in everlasting righteousness, to seal up vision and prophecy and to anoint the most holy."[45] The prophet Daniel spoke these words about the seventy 'sevens' or weeks, but later on, I will discuss the fulfillment of this prophecy. Right now, I want to focus on the events of the prophecy and how they relate to the New Covenant. Whenever this time period of seventy weeks had been fulfilled, then the following events would have occurred: all sin would have been dealt with, there would have been an end to sin, all sin would have been properly atoned for, the ability to prophesy would no longer exist, and we would have been an anointment of everyone into the most holy place. If any one of these events happens, then all of this prophecy would have been fulfilled. When the establishment of the New Covenant occurred, all of these events took place because God promised that he would not remember our sins anymore (consider the passage from Jeremiah).

As I pull all of this information together, the main objective of reading this chapter was to find out the answers to 'how' and 'why' God redeemed Israel from her sin. The whole purpose of the New Covenant was to resolve the separation and bondage of sin. Many events went along with this picture (such as the seventy weeks), but these were trials and tribulations that God chose to send before the restoration of righteousness to his people. Many people get 'caught up' in certain events of the New Testament, but they are missing 'the big picture' of God's design of these two covenants for salvation.

⌘

2.3. The Story of Abraham

When studying the covenantal framework of the Bible, it is crucial to note that the two covenants originated from Abraham's two sons: Isaac and Ishmael. They are offspring of the two covenants mentioned in Galatians 4. Ishmael represents the old covenant, which had fleshly, carnal characteristics. He was the son of Hagar, the slavewoman. On the contrary, Isaac represents the new covenant, which had spiritual characteristics. He was born according to the promise. He is the son of Sarah, the freewoman.

On this chapter, I am going to present the story of Isaac and Ishmael told in Genesis. It is a mere citation of verses from Genesis and "Antiquities of the Jews" written by Josephus, but I am going to make some crucial points as I write along. I hope that the readers will be able to see the significance of these two boys and how they resemble the pattern of two covenants.

The promise of an heir

This story takes place after Abram refused to receive the goods from the king of Sodom.

After this, the word of the Lord came to Abram in a vision:

"Do not be afraid, Abram,
I am your shield,
your very great reward."

But Abram said, "O Sovereign LORD, what can you give me since I remain childless and the one who will inherit my estate is Eliezer of Damascus?" And Abram said, "You have given me no children; so a servant in my household will be my heir."
Then the word of the Lord came to him; "This man will not be your heir, but a son coming from your own body will be your heir." He took him outside and said, "Look up at the heavens and

count the stars — if indeed you can count them." Then he said to him, "So shall your offspring be."

Abram believed the Lord, and he credited it to him as righteousness.[46]

The promise that God made to Abram is the major issue of this particular passage. Remind yourself that God is a covenant-making and covenant-keeping God. God never breaks his promise. However, Sarai, Abram's wife could not possibly believe that she could bear a child. Hence she attempts every possible means under her own power to fulfill God's promise.

Hagar conceived

Now Sarai, Abram's wife, had borne him no children. But she had an Egyptian maidservant named Hagar; so she said to Abram, "The LORD has kept me from having children. Go, sleep with my maidservant; perhaps I can build a family through her."

Abram agreed to what Sarai said. So after Abram had been living in Canaan ten years, Sarai his wife took her Egyptian maidservant Hagar and gave her to her husband to be his wife. He slept with Hagar, and she conceived.[47]

Finally, Abram obtained his offspring, but is the son of Hagar the offspring that God intended to give to Abram? The result of Sarai's lack of faith leads to her own misfortune.

When she knew that she was pregnant, she began to despise her mistress. Then Sarai said to Abram, "You are responsible for the wrong I am suffering. I put my servant in your arms, and now that she knows she is pregnant, she despises me. May the LORD judge between you and me."

"Your servant is in your hands," Abram said. "Do with her whatever you think best." Then Sarai mistreated Hagar; so she fled from her.[48]

Birth of Ishmael

So Hagar bore Abram a son, and Abram gave the name Ishmael to the son she had borne. Abram was eighty-six years old when Hagar bore him Ishmael.[49]

2. Covenantal Perspective

Let us examine this event from the historical perspective. Josephus, the 1st century Jewish historian, wrote:

> … *when this handmaid (Hagar) was with child, she triumphed, and ventured to affront Sarai, as if the dominion were to come to a son to be born of her; but when Abram resigned her into the hand of Sarai to punish her, she contrived to fly away, as not able to bear the instances of Sarai's severity to her; and she entreated God to have compassion on her.*
>
> *Now a divine angel met her, as she was going forward in the wilderness, and bid her return to her master and mistress; for, if she would submit to that wise advice, she would live better hereafter; for that the reason of her being in such a miserable case was this, that she had been ungrateful and arrogant towards her mistress. He also told her, that if she disobeyed God, and went on still in her way, she should perish; but if she would return back, she should become the mother of a son who should reign over that country. These admonitions she obeyed, and returned to her master and mistress, and obtained forgiveness. A little afterwards, she bare Ishmael, which may be interpreted Heard of God, because God had heard his mother's prayer.*[50]

The Covenant confirmed – the promise of Jewish nation

> *When Abram was ninety-nine years old, the LORD appeared to him and said, "I am God Almighty; walk before me and be blameless. I will confirm my covenant between me and you and will greatly increase your numbers."*
>
> *Abram fell facedown, and God said to him, "As for me, this is my covenant with you: You will be the father of many nations. No longer will you be called Abram; your name will be Abraham, for I have made you a father of many nations. I will make you very fruitful; I will make nations of you, and kings will come from you. I will establish my covenant as an everlasting covenant between me and you and your descendants after you for the generations to come, to be your God and the God of your descendants after you. The whole land of Canaan, where you are now an alien, I will give as an everlasting possession to you and your descendants after you; and I will be their God."*[51]

God confirms with Abram – now Abraham – the covenant, which makes Abraham the patriarch of Jewish nation.

39

The Jewish nation begins from this point on. The Abrahamic covenant was a promise of descendants for Abraham. Keep in mind that Abraham still did not obtain a legitimate son, but one through a slavewoman.

The promise of a nation with the land of Canaan was the covenant that Abraham received. However, this covenant was not given for free – as all other covenants. Here's what God says after making a covenant with Abraham.

Then God said to Abraham, "As for you, you must keep my covenant, you and your descendants after you for the generations to come. This is my covenant with you and your descendants after you, the covenant you are to keep: Every male among you shall be circumcised. You are to undergo circumcision, and it will be the sign of the covenant between me and you.[52]

Keeping the covenant was the responsibility that Abraham and his descendants had to take in their part. God gave them the everlasting covenant that enabled them to acquire the whole land of Canaan, if and only if they kept their covenant. In other words, the Jews would lose their inheritance as soon as they break their covenant.

From the post 1st century perspective, it is not difficult to realize that this Abrahamic covenant – even after the annihilation of Jewish nation in AD 70 – has existed. After the fall of Jerusalem in AD 70, the Jews did not possess the land of Canaan until 20th century. However, it does not mean that the everlasting Abrahamic covenant was broken. The fulfillment of the covenant is now spiritual, given to Christians. Christians are the ones who are living in the land that God promised. It is not a literal land, but a spiritual land that God gave us.

Canaan was a type of this land to come, just as David was a type of Christ, or old Jerusalem was typical of the New Jerusalem. The residence of God's people today is in the new earth promised, which is just as spiritual as everything that belongs in it. Of this earth and this inheritance, Jesus spoke in Matthew 5:5: "Blessed are the meek, for they will inherit the earth." In connection with the prophecy of Amos 9:15[53], Christ said, "My sheep listen to my voice; I know them, and they follow me. I give them eternal life, and they shall never perish; no one can snatch them out of my hand."[54] The statement "no one can snatch them out of my hand" is a fulfillment of Amos 9:15. Christians are the true seed of Abraham, and they are planted in Christ Jesus. They have citizenship in a kingdom, which cannot be moved.[55] Concerning this spiritual seed Paul said, "It was not through the law that Abraham and his offspring received the promise that he would be heir of the world, but through the righteousness that comes by faith."[56] What world was promised to Abraham and his seed? Not the one through the law (Canaan), but the one through the Gospel.[57]

Promise of legitimate offspring: Isaac

After making the covenant with Abraham, God promises that Sarai will have a son. Abraham believes that it is impossible, because Sarai is already ninety years old. But everything is possible with God.

God also said to Abraham, "As for Sarai your wife, you are no longer to call her Sarai; her name will be Sarah. I will bless her and will surely give you a son by her. I will bless her so that she will be the mother of nations; kings of peoples will come from her."

Abraham fell facedown; he laughed and said to himself, "Will a son be born to a man a hundred years old? Will Sarah bear a child at the age of ninety?" And Abraham said to God, "If only Ishmael might live under your blessing!"[58]

Obviously Abraham does not realize that everything is possible with God. God re-affirms that Sarah would have a son, and He names him Isaac.

Two promises concerning Isaac and Ishmael

Then God said, "Yes, but your wife Sarah will bear you a son, and you will call him Isaac. I will establish my covenant with him as an everlasting covenant for his descendants after him. And as for Ishmael, I have heard you: I will surely bless him; I will make him fruitful and will greatly increase his numbers. He will be the father of twelve rulers, and I will make him into a great nation. But my covenant I will establish with Isaac, whom Sarah will bear you by this time next year."[59]

41

The two promises given to Abraham's sons were that Isaac would receive the covenant and Ishmael would become a great nation. Indeed, Ishmael had become a great nation. Josephus explains how this promise was fulfilled.

When the lad was grown up, he married a wife, by birth an Egyptian, from whence the mother was herself derived originally. Of this wife were born to Ishmael twelve sons; Nabaioth, Kedar, Abdeel, Mabsam, idumas, Masmaos, Masoss, Chodad, Theman, Jetur, Naphesus, Cadmas. These inhabited all the country from Euphrates to the Red Sea, and called it Nabatene. They are an Arabian nation and name their tribes from these, both because of their own virtue and because of the dignity of Abraham their father.[60]

Sarah's Laughter; Birth of Isaac

The LORD appeared to Abraham near the great trees of Mamre while he was sitting at the entrance to his tent in the heat of the day. Abraham looked up and saw three men standing nearby. When he saw them, he hurried from the entrance of his tent to meet them and bowed low to the ground.[61]

Abraham brought some curds and milk that had been prepared, and set these before them. While they ate, he stood near them under a tree.[62]

"Where is your wife Sarah? They asked him.
"There, in the tent," he said.
Then the LORD said, "I will surely return to you about this time next year, and Sarah your wife will have a son."

Now Sarah was listening at the entrance to the tent, which was behind him. Abraham and Sarah were already old and well advanced in years, and Sarah was past the age of childbearing. So Sarah laughed to herself as she thought, "After I am worn out and my master is old, will I now have this pleasure?"
Then the LORD said to Abraham, "Why did Sarah laugh and say, 'Will I really have a child, now that I am old?' Is anything too hard for the LORD? I will return to you at the appointed time next year and Sarah will have a son."
Sarah was afraid, so she lied and said, "I did not laugh."

But he said, "Yes, you did laugh."[63]

Now in a little time Abraham had a son by Sarah, as God had foretold to him, whom he named Isaac, which signifies Laughter; and indeed they so called him, because Sarah laughed when God said that she should bear a son, she not expecting such a thing, as being past the age of childbearing, for she was ninety years old, and Abraham an hundred; so that this son was born to them both in the last year of each of those decimal numbers. And they circumcised him upon the eighth day.[64]

Expulsion of Ishmael

Now a misfortune occurs on Hagar and Ishmael. Sarah decides to drive out those two from Abraham's household. Josephus explains why she decided to do so.

> *As for Sarah, she at first loved Ishmael, who was born of her own handmaid Hagar, with an affection not inferior to that of her own son, for he was brought up, in order to succeed in the government; but when she herself had borne Isaac, she was not willing that Ishmael should be brought up with him, as being too old for him, and able to do him injuries when their father should be dead; she therefore persuaded Abraham to send him and his mother to some distant country.*[65]
>
> *Now, at the first he did not agree to what Sarah was so zealous for, and thought it an instance of the greatest barbarity to send away a young child and a woman unprovided of necessaries; but at length he agreed to it; because God was pleased with what Sarah had determined; so he delivered Ishmael to his mother, as not yet able to go by himself; and commanded her to take a bottle of water, and a loaf of bread, and so to depart, and to take Necessity for her guide.*[66]

It was not out of mere hatred that Sarah decided to drive out Hagar and Ishmael, but because she knew that two sons could not share the same inheritance. That's what God had in mind, too. One had to be cast out. The Bible gives another account concerning the same issue:

> *The child grew and was weaned, and on the day Isaac was*

weaned Abraham held a great feast. But Sarah saw that the son whom Hagar the Egyptian had borne to Abraham was mocking, and she said to Abraham, "Get rid of that slave woman and her son, for that slave woman's son will never share in the inheritance with my son Isaac."

The matter distressed Abraham greatly because it concerned his son. But God said to him, "Do not be so distressed about the boy and your maidservant. Listen to whatever Sarah tells you, because it is through Isaac that your offspring will be reckoned. I will make the son of the maidservant into a nation also, because he is your offspring.

Early the next morning Abraham took some food and a skin of water and gave them to Hagar. He set them on her shoulders and then sent her off with the boy. She went on her way and wandered in the desert of Beersheba.[67]

Finally, Ishmael and Hagar are cast out. The reason why they were to be cast out is because God intended to give the inheritance to Isaac. But why only Isaac? Note that Isaac was born through promise, while Ishmael was born according to human will. It would be hard to believe that this event was a pattern of the things to come. However, the relationship between two boys was a pattern of the two covenants that were to come; the old and new covenant. The old covenant being the Law of Moses, and the new covenant being fulfilled in Christ. Just as the boys coexisted in the same household for a certain period of time, so will the two covenants coexist together. The transition period between the two covenants, when both coexisted, will be dealt heavily in the next chapter, 'the Transfer of Covenants.'

⌘

2.4. Transfer of Covenants

Once we have learned the covenantal basics of God's message, then you will proceed to discover how God transferred his people from the first covenant to the next. This transition was not easy for the people of the early Christian age, and it made an enormous impact on where they were found every Sunday morning. We will discuss the urgency of the Gospel within this early Christian era; the basics of covenants will help display the transition that peaked at the ending of the Old Covenant.

In order to analyze this topic, it is important to think about when each covenant began. Everyone would probably agree that the Old Covenant began at God's deliverance of the Ten Commandments to Moses[68] because this was the first time that mankind received a literal law. Also, another thing to consider is when the New Covenant began. Jesus announced the beginning of process taking place at the Lord's Supper[69] (Around AD 30), but nothing had been established until everything was complete (Remember: the Lord's Supper was before the crucifixion of Christ, resurrection of Christ, and Pentecost Day). Before the collapse of the headquarters and the house of God's presence in the Old Covenant (Jerusalem and her temple) in AD 70, Israel's original covenant was still intact. Judaism was still a valid religion until the New Covenant was firmly consummated at the fall of Jerusalem. This is contrary to popular belief about the Old Covenant's expiration, and this Biblical contradiction can be proved in Hebrews 8:13, "By calling this covenant "new," he has made the first one obsolete; and what is obsolete and aging will soon disappear." Historically, the book of Hebrews was written many years after Jesus' resurrection, but the book of Hebrews tells us that this obsolete covenant will SOON disappear.

If this plain, single verse does not convince you that the Old Covenant ended at the fall of Jerusalem (or had not disappeared after Christ's resurrection), then we will study Galatians

4:21-31. In this passage, Paul contrasts both covenants in an allegorical (story that is symbolic for another story) method that represents Abraham's two sons. Let the study begin: "Tell me, you who want to be under the law, are you not aware of what the law says? For it is written that Abraham had two sons, one by the slave woman and the other by the free woman. His son by the slave woman was born in the ordinary way; but his son by the free woman was born as the result of a promise."[70] As we will learn later on in the passage, these two sons represent two covenants. What have we already stated in previous chapters about people who lived under the Old Covenant? They were enslaved to sin, and people who are under the New Covenant are set free this bondage that caused spiritual death. Continuing the passage from Galatians, Paul says, "These things may be taken figuratively, for the women represent two covenants. One covenant is from Mount Sinai and bears children who are to be slaves: This is Hagar. Now Hagar stands for Mount Sinai in Arabia and corresponds to the present city of Jerusalem, because she is in slavery with her children."[71] Hagar was a literal slave, which was a pattern of those Jews who were spiritual slaves. The Jewish slavery was established at Mount Sinai (Mount Sinai was where God gave the Ten Commandments to Moses, and he established the Old Covenant). Notice that Paul says that the current city of Jerusalem (Paul's current city, not Jerusalem today) are still slaves. How would this be possible if sin's bondage (Old Covenant) had already been destroyed in the past? The Old Covenant's death (separation from God) had not been destroyed because of the future tense presented in 1 Corinthians 15:26: "The last enemy to be destroyed is death."

As we read further in the scripture, "But the Jerusalem that is above is free, and she is our mother. For it is written: "Be glad, O barren woman, who bears no children; break forth and cry aloud, you who have no labor pains; because more are the children of the desolate woman than of her who has a husband." Now you, brothers, like Isaac, are children of promise."[72] In comparison, there was a literal Jerusalem in Judea, which is known to be the Old Jerusalem because it was the house of God in the Old Covenant. But this verse talks about another Jerusalem that is spiritual (or above) which is in the opposite of the Old Jerusalem, because it is free. A description of this New Jerusalem was prophesied by Isaiah: "In that day

46

this song will be sung in the land of Judah: We have a strong city; God makes salvation its walls and ramparts."[73] This city is strong, and it is totally different from the original, weak city, in which the Jews thought that the old Jerusalem's literal walls could protect them from the Roman army. In the strong city, no man or being will be able to tear down the relationship with God because we have received the guaranteed inheritance of salvation.

As the allegory continues: "At that time the son born in the ordinary way persecuted the son born by the power of the Spirit. It is the same now. But what does the Scripture say? "Get rid of the slave woman and her son, for the slave woman's son will never share in the inheritance with the free woman's son." Therefore, brothers, we are not children of the slave woman, but of the free woman."[74] The first verse describes the trials or tribulations that the Christians (those born of the promise), and Jesus told the apostles about this tribulation in his sermon at the Mount of Olives (Olivet Discourse): "But before all this, they will lay hands on you and persecute you. They will deliver you to synagogues and prisons, and you will be brought before kings and governors, and all on account of my name…You will be betrayed even by parents, brothers, relatives and friends, and they will put some of you to death. All men will hate you because of me."[75] Notice it mentions synagogues (place of worship for the Jews); Saul (Paul's old self or name before becoming a Christian) was one of the Jewish persecutors that had the authority from the governors and kings to persecute Christians. These verses described most of the historic trials of the apostles, and this is why Jesus warned them directly. But referring back to the allegory, God cast out the slave woman and her son, and they did not share in the inheritance of God's promise. In the covenantal perspective, how could the Old Covenant be cast out without it coexisting with the New Covenant? This is why that I believe that fall of Jerusalem was such a significant event because it was where God dwelled, and it was time that God removed his people from focusing on geography and kings to his ministry of the Spirit. In the coming chapters, we will discuss the historical account of the fall of Jerusalem, and how it was the most devastating event in history. Hopefully, this terrorizing event will help us understand how this event would be the mark of the casting out of the bond woman and her son.

From the beginning of Jesus' New Covenant Ministry (Lord's Supper in about AD 30) to the end of the Old Covenant (Fall of Jerusalem in AD 70), there was a forty-year period of time, which I label as 'The Forty Years of Wandering'. This is also known as to be a 'Grace Period' that God gave to the Jews so that they could gradually turn toward Christ before God judged Israel and her fleshly covenant. As probably all of us can remember in the story of Moses, the Red Sea parted and they were released from their slavery from Egypt, but 40 years of wandering took place. They, finally, reached their destination in 'The Promised Land'. God had to guide them every step of the way out of Egypt in order for them to finally reach the beloved land of Canaan. If you remember, Canaan was the land that Jacob obtained before Joseph ran off into Egypt. Canaan was once Israel's land; God mercifully restored their land after a long period of slavery and wandering. This same story applies to the coexisting covenants, the early Christians had the guarantee of sacrifice after the cross, but until the Old Covenant had been dealt with, these Christians still needed God's guidance to point them in the direction of spiritual restoration. Remember, until the seventy weeks of Daniel were fulfilled, there was not a complete establishment of the New Covenant because the New Covenant's purpose was to deal with sin.

In order to learn more in depth about Jesus' deliverance of sin, we will be studying Romans 5:12-21. This allegory brings more clarity of Jesus' deliverance of sin in opposition to Adam's deliverance of separation from God: "Therefore, just as sin entered the world through one man, and death through sin, and in this way death came to all men, because all sinned--for before the law was given, sin was in the world. But sin is not taken into account when there is no law. Nevertheless, death reigned from the time of Adam to the time of Moses, even over those who did not sin by breaking a command, as did Adam, who was a pattern of the one to come. But the gift is not like the trespass. For if the many died by the trespass of the one man, how much more did God's grace and the gift that came by the grace of the one man, Jesus Christ, overflow to the many! Again, the gift of God is not like the result of the one man's sin: The judgment followed one sin and brought condemnation, but the gift followed many trespasses and brought justification. For if, by the trespass of the one man, death reigned through that one man, how much more will those who receive God's abundant provision of grace and of the gift of righteousness reign in life through the one man, Jesus Christ. Consequently, just as the result of one trespass was condemnation for all men, so also the result of one act of righteousness was justification that brings life for all men. For just as through the disobedience of the one man the many were made sinners, so also through the obedience of the one man the many will be made righteous. The law was added so that the trespass might increase. But where sin increased, grace increased all the more, so that, just as sin reigned in death, so also grace might reign through righteousness to bring eternal life through Jesus Christ our Lord."[76]

Adam was an imperfect sinner, and his one sin brought condemnation and death to the rest of humanity for future generations. When Moses came along, God decided to give the Old Testament people an opportunity to escape from spiritual death. In the beginning of these laws, God made it seem simple to bring self-justification, but still every man attempted to keep those ten laws and failed. Another man whose name was Jesus brought life into the world[77] by his own power. Just like Adam made everyone else perishable, dishonorable, weak, and a salvation that was realistically impossible to obtain, Jesus made everyone else imperishable, glorious, strong, and he gave them a real salvation. After God's establishment of New Covenant, God's grace flooded, and he covered all of sin through his son. As it says in Hebrews 9:25-26: "Nor did he enter heaven to offer himself again and again, the way the high priest enters the Most Holy Place every year with blood that is not his own. Then Christ would have had to suffer many times since the creation of the world. But now he has appeared once for all at the end of the ages to do away with sin by the sacrifice of himself." There is no way the Most Holy Place (Place for atonement for sin) in Daniel 9:24 could be anointed without the destruction of the old, physical one: "The Holy Spirit was showing by this that the way into the Most Holy Place had not yet been disclosed as long as the first tabernacle was still standing." The tabernacle (or tent) of the Old Testament was a mobile sin offering facility. Since this verse was referring to its present time, it is reasonable to assume that it was referring to the stationary facility for sin offering in Jerusalem. This verse proves that until the Temple in Jerusalem or Old Covenant had been destroyed, the anointed Most Holy Place in Daniel 9:24 could not be entered by God's people before the completion and casting out of the Old Covenant.

As this chapter comes to a close, it may be useful to reread this chapter and/or these verses to discover the truth of how the covenants coexisted for a forty-year period of time. This fact is highly crucial in order for you to understand the remaining elements of the book. If you are not with us on this page, then it is highly recommended to do some independent study about the covenantal transition. The points have been presented, and now, it is time for you to decide whether or not you agree with the points presented. If everything is ready to go, and you agree with everything said, then I suggest reading the next chapter as the excitement of understanding the Bible continues.

⌘

3. First Century Christianity and Judaism

3.1. Two Audiences for Ministry

There were different groups that received the gospel during the forty-year transitional period of time. If we still do not understand this fact about the two groups that would receive that gospel in two entirely different perspectives, then this chapter will be more comprehensive in attempting to understand these areas of ministry. We will study how these two groups: Jews and Gentiles played different roles in the reception of early Christianity. Hopefully, as we began to study scripture, we will begin to realize why there was a forty-year grace period.

The Jews were very restrictive in their ministry, and they were still very zealous (observant) of the law after the cross. This very subject seems highly intriguing as to why the Holy Spirit did not automatically convince the Jews that their law (Old Covenant) had regulations that no longer existed. The major issue that was discussed among the Jews was circumcision. The first time that Peter took action in accepting the uncircumcised (Gentiles) was:

While Peter was still speaking these words, the Holy Spirit came on all who heard the message. The circumcised believers who had come with Peter were astonished that the gift of the Holy Spirit had been poured out even on the Gentiles. For they heard them speaking in tongues and praising God. Then Peter said, "Can anyone keep these people from being baptized with water? They have received the Holy Spirit just as we have." So he ordered that they be baptized in the name of Jesus Christ. Then they asked Peter to stay with them for a few days.[78]

This was a direct reaction of Peter's vision that was explained earlier in this chapter[79]. Listen to how the reaction was of the whole crowd of men in Jerusalem: "The apostles and the brothers throughout Judea heard that the Gentiles also had received the word of God. So when Peter went up to Jerusalem, the circumcised believers criticized him and said:

You went into the house of uncircumcised men and ate with them.[80]

As you can see, the Judaizers of the time were not too comfortable with Peter for participating in these actions. What the Judaizers did not realize is that God gave approval for Peter to baptize these Gentiles, because otherwise the Holy Spirit would have not given them the gifts to speak in tongues. After Peter explains[81] his actions, the Judaizers began to see in the scripture:

When they heard this, they had no further objections and praised God, saying, "So then, God has granted even the Gentiles repentance unto life."[82]

Notice, that they had to go through a logical process of explaining before they accepted the true message of God with no hesitation. This simple fact can be applied to several elements of Peter's ministry in that it did not happen automatically as some of us tend to think. Also today, when we know that there is truth in a matter, then we must provide a logical explanation of the subject before we automatically assume that the other person knows of this truth.

Moving along in the scripture, this controversial subject was finally discussed within the council in Jerusalem, and the problem was stated in Acts 15:1:

Some men came down from Judea to Antioch and were teaching the brothers: "Unless you are circumcised, according to the custom taught by Moses, you cannot be saved."

This caused severe conflict among the Jews and Gentiles, and they established an elite gathering to discuss this subject. During this discussion, Peter made a very interesting point:

After much discussion, Peter got up and addressed them: "Brothers, you know that some time ago God made a choice among you that the Gentiles might hear from my lips the message of the gospel and believe. God, who knows the heart, showed that he accepted them by giving the Holy Spirit to them, just as he did to us. He made no distinction between us and them, for he purified their hearts by faith. Now then, why do you try to test God by putting on the necks of the disciples a yoke that neither we nor our fathers have been able to bear? No! We believe it is through the grace of our Lord Jesus that we are saved, just as they are."[83]

The statement that seemed so significant was when he

3. First Century Christianity and Judaism

talked about how none of their fathers could bear the yolk (or enslavement) of the law. He admitted that no one person could justify himself through his obedience to the law, and the reason that this seems interesting is: 'why was it that the Gentiles were the only ones that did not have to obey the law?' If you read about the council of Jerusalem in Acts chapter, it is obvious they did not want to decide any details about the future of Jewish Christians, and whether or not they should participate in circumcision in the future. The reason is because Peter's ministry had not completed in weaning them away from their roots of Jewish tradition.

Another interesting figure was Paul's niche as an apostle in first century Christianity because while he was leaving Ephesus, he was inspired by the Holy Spirit to venture to Jerusalem[84]. Although Paul was warned by others not to go to Jerusalem because of forward trouble[85], he had a very strong conviction that it was God's will for him go to Jerusalem[86]. So the next day, James and the elders of Jerusalem greeted Paul, and he participated in Jewish purification rites[87] so that the Jews would know that Paul was still zealous for the law[88]. Now that the historical events are set into place, the question would be: Why was it God's will for Paul to participate in purification rites that proved that he was obedient to a law that he later condemns[89] in his ministry to the Gentiles? Was it for the simple reason so that Jews would have more respect for Paul, or does it contain deeper significance? According to traditional belief that the Old Covenant ended at the cross, why would God influence Paul to participate in a religion that had no validity? The only justified answer is that God was giving the Jews a grace period of forty years to allow them to participate in their traditions, but as the Bible says:

But what does the Scripture say? "Get rid of the slave woman and her son, for the slave woman's son will never share in the inheritance with the free woman's son."[90]

These Jews were given the testimony of Jesus Christ after his crucifixion, but when would it be too late for Paul to participate in these purification rites? Paul understood that the Jewish Covenant was going to end[91], and it was acceptable for them to be still zealous for the law for a certain period of time. Until the process of weaning them away from the law was complete, Paul would approve of Jewish Christianity.

Paul's main audience of ministry was not of the Jews, but

it was for the Gentiles. In Galatia, Paul tells them who asked him about observing the law:

You foolish Galatians! Who has bewitched you? Before your very eyes Jesus Christ was clearly portrayed as crucified. I would like to learn just one thing from you: Did you receive the Spirit by observing the law, or by believing what you heard? Are you so foolish? After beginning with the Spirit, are you now trying to attain your goal by human effort? Have you suffered so much for nothing--if it really was for nothing? Does God give you his Spirit and work miracles among you because you observe the law, or because you believe what you heard?[92]

Paul deliberately persuades them not to observe the law, and asks them why they want to become like the Jews of the time. The reason that Paul does not promote law observant among the Gentiles is because they were not born in Jewish tradition, and if they were to obtain complete observance, then that would be a substantial step backwards in the Apostle's ministry to wean everyone away from the law. The reason that some of the Galatians decided to participate in the activities of the law was because Jews told the Galatians and other Gentiles that they had to be circumcised in order to be saved.[93]

This was one great dilemma of the 1st Century events; the book of Acts relates to both ministries in order to tell the story of the process for the Jews to become Christians. In my mind, if God just told the Jews abruptly after the cross that they had to discontinue all customs because of Christ, then I do not think that there would have been as many conversions of the 1st century when taking that scenario. In what other way could the Jews have been converted and still discontinue their activities of Jewish practices? I cannot think of any other, and this is why God's reasoning is supreme to in of our petty knowledge because if some of us would have it our way, then the nation of Israel would have not been considered members of the early church. Although it is not to say that there was no end to Judaism, Jesus predicted this end of everything the apostles would have valued living in their present age, and we will begin to understand in later chapters what it meant to live in the 'age to come'. As we think about the process advancing in the 1st Century age, there would be a dawn of a new age and an end to an old age.

⌘

3.2. Great Commission

In 1976, the bimillennial movement found its first major convert among the Southern Baptists. In keeping with their evangelical zeal, they launched a plan "to reach every living person in the world with the gospel by the year 2000." Dubbed "Bold Mission Thrust" this daring and detailed strategy called for a tenfold increase of churches worldwide by the year 2000.[94] It has been 24 years from then. Did they reach every living person in the world with the gospel by the year 2000, literally?

Many churches claim that the Great Commission given by Christ is yet unfulfilled. This commission is mentioned in Matthew 24:14 – and in other gospels as well; "This good news of the kingdom will be proclaimed throughout the world, as a testimony to all the nations; and then the end will come". It is used often to acknowledge the fact that the second coming will not take place until the gospel is preached to all nations. This was a sign given to the disciples by Jesus, that the end would come after the Great Commission is fulfilled.

In order to realize the true meaning of the Great Commission and the fulfillment, one should understand that the prophecy is to be viewed from the 1st century perspective rather than the 20th century one. Note that the Bible is a 1st century version, not a 20th century version. There are two questions to think about. Did the apostles know the world that we know today, and could the 'nations' have different meaning figuratively than from our 20th century perspective?

First, there are a list of verses that use the same style of writing as 'all nations', and 'throughout the world' in Mattthew 24:14:

Colossians 1:5-6

"*- You have heard of this hope before in the word of the truth, the gospel that has come to you. Just as it is bearing fruit*

57

and growing in the whole world, so it has been bearing fruit among yourselves from the day you heard it and truly compre- hended the grace of God."

If the "world" mentioned in Matthew 24:14 meant the "world" we know today, then Paul is making a false statement here, because the gospel had been preached to several nations in eastern Mediterranean, but not the whole world that we know today. Thus, the "world" must have been the Mediterra- nean world under Rome that the 1st century Christians knew.

Note that the Olivet Discourse which was recorded in Matthew 24 took place even before the crucifixion of Christ while the letter to Colossians was written around 60 AD.

Romans 9:17

"For the scripture says to Pharaoh, "I have raised you up for the very purpose of showing my power in you, so that my name may be proclaimed in ALL THE EARTH."

This verse indicates that this language doesn't mean liter- ally the planet earth, but "the earth", which could be defined as "soil", "ground", or "land". It is simply a language used figura- tively – the point is that not all the verses are to be taken liter- ally, and that Matthew 24:14 should not be taken literally.

Acts 1:8

"But you will receive power when the Holy Spirit has come upon you; and you will be my witnesses in Jerusalem, in all Judea and Samaria, and to the ends of the earth."

This verse is a part of Christ's response to the disciples when they asked him whether it was time He would restore the Kingdom to Israel. Did the apostles become Christ's witnesses to THE ENDS OF THE EARTH literally? No, but rather figuratively. This is another proof of spiritual interpretation over the literal one.

Acts 2:5

"Now there were devout Jews from EVERY NATION UNDER HEAVEN living in Jerusalem."

3. First Century Christianity and Judaism

The word "nation" may be interpreted as the twelve tribes of Israel, or it can rather be meant as the every nation of the world – the Mediterranean world, that the apostles knew that time. It could be also suggested that there were Jews from the whole world that we know today, but there isn't any biblical support for this statement.

Luke 2:1

"In those days a decree went out from Emperor Augustus that ALL THE WORLD should be registered."

This is another proof that the writers of the gospels had a perspective of the world different than the 20th century perspective.

So far, all the verses listed above simply supported the fact that the words "all the nations", or "the ends of the earth" should not have been taken literally. Some might still say that for Matthew 24:14's case, the definition of the "world" was literally the entire modern world that we know today. However, what if the Bible says that the gospel had already been preached? Here are the verses that prove this statement.

Colossians 1:23

"provided that you continue securely established and steadfast in the faith, without shifting from the hope promised by the gospel that you heard, <u>which has been proclaimed to every creation under heaven.</u> I, Paul, became a servant of this gospel."

It says in text that the gospel had been preached! Just compare the time of Olivet Discourse (AD 30s) and the time when this letter was written (AD 60s).

Romans 1:8

"First, I thank my God through Jesus Christ for all of you, because <u>your faith is proclaimed throughout the world.</u>"

This is another verse with a similar language as Colossians 1:23.

Romans 10:18

"But I ask, have they (1) not heard? Indeed they have; for "Their (2) voice has gone out to all the earth, and their words to the ends of the world.""

They (1) are the ones who have not obeyed the good news (10:16), they are the Jews. Right after v.18, Paul states in v.19, "Again I ask, did Israel not understand?"

Their (2); they are the ones who bring good news as mentioned in v.15. Their voice and words have gone to all the earth and to the ends of the world, Paul says. Thus, Matthew 24:14 had already been fulfilled by the time Paul wrote his letter to the Romans.

Romans 16:25-26

"Now to God who is able to strengthen you according to my gospel and the proclamation of Jesus Christ, according to the revelation of the mystery that was kept secret for long ages but is now disclosed, and through the prophetic writings is made known to all the Gentiles, according to the command of the eternal God, through Jesus Christ, to whom be glory forever! Amen."

From the contemporary literal interpretation, this statement is false. The Bible says that the revelation is made known to all the Gentiles. From the 20th century perspective, this may seem to be a false statement. However, according to the spiritual interpretation, this is a correct statement.

Therefore, the Great Commission had already been fulfilled by the time these letters were written. Jesus clearly said in Matthew 24:14, that the end would come soon after the gospel had been preached to all the nations. The Great Commission had already been fulfilled in 1st century. Now what? Are we waiting for the end to come?

⌘

3.3. Holy Spirit and the Last Days

"Love never fails. But where there are prophecies, they will cease; where there are tongues, they will be stilled; where there is knowledge, it will pass away. For we know in part and we prophesy in part, but when perfection comes, the imperfect disappears."

1 Corinthians 13:8-10

One supernatural phenomenon, or rather the series of infinite phenomena, was mostly involved with the workings of the Holy Spirit. This was another 1ˢᵗ century element that we do not possess today. The Holy Spirit was given to the church while Christ was absent. It was a comforter, a counselor, or an advocate.

The Holy Spirit came to the church when Peter gave the Pentecostal sermon to the ministry, after Christ was lifted up to heaven. Coming of the Holy Spirit was an apocalyptic sign, which Joel prophesied:

And afterwards, I will pour out my Spirit on all people. Your sons and daughters will prophesy, your old men will dream dreams, your young men will see visions. Even on my servants, both men and women, I will pour out my Spirit in those days. I will show wonders in the heavens and on the earth, blood and fire and billows of smoke. The sun will be turned to darkness and the moon to blood before the coming of the great and dreadful day of the LORD. And everyone who calls on the name of the LORD will be saved; for on Mount Zion and in Jerusalem there will be a deliverance, as the LORD has said, among the survivors whom the LORD calls.95

Receiving of the Holy Spirit announced that the last days had come.[96] This sign also brought spiritual gifts such as speaking in tongues, an ability to prophesy, miracles, knowledge, etc. We know that such elements existed in the 1ˢᵗ century; in Christ, the 1ˢᵗ century Christians were enriched in every way – in all their speaking and in all their knowledge.[97] Paul writes to the church in Corinth, "Therefore you do not lack any spiritual gift as you eagerly wait for our Lord Jesus Christ to be revealed."[98] The 1ˢᵗ century Christians held on to their eschatological expectation of Christ's return, and they had these spiritual gifts which helped them to be firmly established in the new covenant as it was in process of its consummation.

This Holy Spirit also had a purpose of showing what was in process – the resurrection to confirm who God's sons were. Such distinction was necessary between the old covenant men and the new covenant men. People were baptized in the Holy Spirit to become a part of the church. It was a deposit that guaranteed what Peter mentions:

...an inheritance that can never perish, spoil or fade – kept in heaven for you, who through faith are shielded by God's power until the coming of the salvation that is ready to be revealed in the last time.[99]

Many Christians today claim that they have inheritance and God's salvation, however, according to Peter's statement above, their claims are invalid. Concerning the same subject, Paul wrote:

And you also were included in Christ when you heard the word of truth, the gospel of your salvation. Having believed, you were marked in him with a seal, the promised Holy Spirit, who is **a deposit guaranteeing our inheritance** *until the redemption of those who are God's possession – to the praise of his glory.*[100]

He said to them, "Go into all the world and preach the good news to all creation. Whoever believes and is baptized will be saved, but whoever does not believe will be condemned. And these signs will accompany those who believe: In my name they will drive out demons; they will speak in new tongues; they will pick up snakes with their hands; and when they drink deadly poison, it will not hurt them at all; they will place their hands on sick people, and they will get well."[101]

I'd like to know how many Christians there are, who tried all those things that Christ spoke of, if there's any single one at all. Everyone who has the gift of Holy Spirit should be able to do it, but we can't. Why? Did Jesus use hyperbole in that passage? No, for in the 1st century things that he spoke of took place literally. Then, for what reason do we lack these abilities that would be so helpful in preaching the gospel message to non-Christians? There must've been a significant event that changed the ground for these conditions for which they had been possible.

Our contemporary Christians claim that we have the Holy Spirit and God's salvation, redemption, etc. At the same time, we deny the supernatural forces involved with being a Christian; we claim that those things were only pertained to the 1st century Christians. Yet, the 1st century Christians had the ability because they were living in the last days. Then the question finally comes down to: "Are we still living in the last days?"

⌘

3.4. Jewish Atonement

The old covenant's weakness was that a person could not be separated from sin due to the fact that nobody could observe the law perfectly. Once they committed sin by disobeying the law, the old covenant man separated himself from God. The sin could never be separated from man as long as he remained under the old covenant. Paul pointed out this problem in his letter to Corinthians concerning the fact that the sin had to do with the old law: "The sting of death is sin, and the power of sin is the law."[102]

This may confuse readers to believe that the old law was sinful or unholy, but the old covenant was not sin itself. Paul explains how the sin worked under the old law.

What shall we say, then? Is the law sin? Certainly not! Indeed I would not have known what sin was except through the law. For I would not have known what coveting really was if the law had not said, "Do not covet." But sin, seizing the opportunity afforded by the commandment, produced in me every kind of covetous desire. For apart from law sin is dead. Once I was alive apart from law; but when the commandment came, sin sprang to life and I died. I found that the very commandment that was intended to bring life actually brought death. For sin, seizing the opportunity afforded by the commandment, deceived me, and through the commandment put me to death.[103]

Sin had an opportunity to bring death to people under the old covenant. Without the cleansing of sin, God could not dwell among the Israelites and they certainly could not call themselves as God's chosen people. In order to cleanse the sin they committed throught a year, the Jews gathered over the temple on the day of the atonement to cleanse their sins that

65

they unintentionally committed.

Before dealing with the old Levitical atonement, we'll briefly study how the sanctuary looked like back in the Old Testament period.

Now the first covenant had regulations for worship and also an earthly sanctuary. A tabernacle was set up. In its first room were the lampstand, the table and the consecrated bread; this was was called the Holy Place. Behind the second curtain was a room called the Most Holy Place, which had the golden altar of incense and the gold-covered ark of the covenant. This ark contained the gold jar of manna, Aaron's staff that had budded, and the stone tablets of the covenant. Above the ark were the cherubim of the Glory, overshadowing the atonement cover. But we cannot discuss these things in detail now.[104]

The Day of the Atonement

The most solemn day of the year was the fast of Yom Kippur, the Day of Atonement, when the high priest himself administered all Temple services and went before the LORD to offer atonement for the sins of the nation. Although it was not one of the ordained pilgrim festivals, Yom Kippur preceded Succoth by only five days, and so many Jews assembled in Jerusalem for both the fast and the feast.

For this critically important service, the high priest had to prepare with great care. To avoid the possibility of ritual impurity, he would leave his home and enter a special apartment in the Temple seven days before the Day of Atonement. During this week, every step of the prescribed ritual would be studied and renewed in detail, for it was of utmost importance that no mistake be made. On the night before the service, he would maintain a vigil in the company of several other priests, who would read Scripture with him and help him to stay awake. Meanwhile, in case anything should happen to him, another priest was also being made ready to take his place.

The high priest wore special vestments for Yom Kippur, and in the course of the long day of ritual he would change them several times, bathing 5 times and washing his hands and feet 10 times. Early in the ritual, he would ceremoniously cast lots to choose between two goats – one to be offered as a burnt sacrifice, the other to be driven into the fearsome Judean Wilderness to die as a "scapegoat." He would confess that he himself had committed sins and would sacrifice a young bull as an offering for those sins and for the collective sins of all priests.

Then, as the people followed his movements in apprehensive silence, fearful that he and they would be met with divine wrath, he would make his annual entrance into the Holy of Holies, there – in the name of all Israel and on their behalf – to offer atonement in the presence of God. Three times the high priest would go into the empty room, wherein, it was believed, God's presence would be made manifest, and at each reemergence, the people would breathe a collective sigh of relief. The first time, he would make an offering of incense, filling the room with aromatic smoke. The second time, he would sprinkle the chamber with some of the blood of the young bull he had sacrificed earlier. Before his third and final entry he would sacrifice the goat that had been chosen for the purpose, and then he would sprinkle the chamber with some of the goat's blood.

Returning to the altar, the high priest would then lay his hands on the scapegoat and make confession for all the people, transferring their sins onto the animal. At the end of each confession – he would speak the LORD's name aloud – the only time the hallowed word could properly be spoken. Then the people formed a pathway through which another priest led the scapegoat toward the desert. It was taken to a deep ravine some 12 miles from Jerusalem, and there pushed over a steep cliff. The news of the animal's death was relayed by signals back to the high priest, and after he had performed a few final ceremonies, the day was concluded with great rejoicing. Atonement had been made for the year; it was time to go back home and try with renewed faith and determination to live truly by the laws of God.[105]

This detailed explanation is summed up in both the Old Testament and New Testament. I'll emphasize the significance of the Day of Atonement. It is quoted from the Old Testament, book of Leviticus: "He shall then slaughter the goat for the sin offering for the people and take its blood behind the curtain and do with it as he did with the bull's blood: He shall sprinkle it on the atonement cover and in front of it. In this way he will make atonement for the Most Holy Place because of the uncleanness and rebellion of the Israelites, whatever their sins have been. He is to do the same for the Tent of Meeting, which is among them in the midst of their uncleanness. No one is to be in the Tent of Meeting from the time Aaron goes in to make atonement in the Most Holy Place until he comes out, having made atonement for himself, his household and the whole community of Israel."[106]

Despite the efforts made by the Israelites, the old covenantal atonement was not perfect, and it was the reason why the atonement had to be done every year. Here's another account from the letter to Hebrews from the New Testament.

When everything had been arranged like this, the priests entered regularly into the outer room to carry on their ministry. But only the high priest entered the inner room, and that only once a year, and never without blood, which he offered for himself and for the sins the people had committed in ignorance. The Holy Spirit was showing that the way into the Most Holy Place has not yet been disclosed as long as the first tabernacle was still standing. This is an illustration for the present time, indicating that the gifts and sacrifices being offered were not able to clear the conscience of the worshipper. They are only a matter of food and drink and various ceremonial washings – external regulations applying until the time of the new order.[107]

This atonement had to be done every year, but everything changed after Christ came. Christ, being the High Priest of God brought us the new covenantal atonement under which our sins are forgiven. The difference between the old and new atonement is that while one is temporal, another is permanent. It is crucial to study about the atonement because it is how we obtained our salvation in Jesus Christ. This new atonement and its significance will be dealt with in later chapter, "the Atonemental Perspective of Revelation".

⌘

4. The Fall of Jerusalem

4.1. Martyr of Stephen

Whereas the war which the Jews made with the Romans hath been the greatest of all those, not only that have been in our times, but, in a manner, of those that ever were heard of; both of those wherein cities have fought against cities, or nations against nations

Josephus, the Wars of the Jews

Stephen was the first saint to be martyred in the history of Christianity. He was a man full of God's grace and power, and he performed great wonders and miraculous signs among the people.[108] The opposition arose. The Jews, who plotted to kill him, seized Stephen. Stephen attempted to reason with the Jews, but his words angered the Jews even more. Following are the words that he said before he was stoned.

However, the Most High does not live in houses made by men. As the prophet says: 'Heaven is my throne, and the earth is my footstool. What kind of house will you build for me? Says the Lord. Or where will my resting-place be? Has not my hand made all these things?'

You stiff-necked people, with uncircumcised hearts and ears! You are just like your fathers: You always resist the Holy Spirit! Was there ever a prophet your fathers did not persecute? They even killed those who predicted the coming of the Righteous One. And now you have betrayed and murdered him – you who have received the law that was put into effect through angels but have not obeyed it.[109]

Soon after hearing this, the mob rushed at him and stoned him to death. This was the first martyrdom, and since then the Jews began to pile up their iniquities. After few decades, Paul wrote the hardships Christians struggled through

71

in his letter to Thessalonians. "For you, brothers, became imitators of God's churches in Judea, which are in Christ Jesus: You suffered from your own countrymen the same things those churches suffered from the Jews, who killed the Lord Jesus and the prophets and also drove us out. They displease God and are hostile to all men in their effort to keep us from speaking to the Gentiles so that they may be saved. In this way they always heap up their sins to the limit. The wrath of God has come upon them at last."[110]

The Jews were to be punished for their sins. Jesus said to the Pharisees, "Woe to you, teachers of the law and Pharisees, you hypocrites! You build tombs for the prophets and decorate the graves of the righteous. And you say, 'If we had lived in the days of our forefathers, we would not have taken part with them in shedding the blood of the prophets.' So you testify against yourselves that you are the descendants of those who murdered the prophets. Fill up, then, the measure of the sin of your forefathers!

You snakes! You brood of vipers! How will you escape being condemned to hell? Therefore I am sending you prophets and wise men and teachers. Some of them you will kill and crucify; others you will flog in your synagogues and pursue from town to town. And so upon you will come all the righteous blood that has been shed on earth, from the blood of righteousness Abel to the blood of Zechariah son of Berekiah, who you murdered between the temple and the altar. I tell you the truth, all this will come upon this generation."[111]

Nearly forty years before the fall of Jerusalem, Jesus and apostles already knew that the Jews were to be punished for their iniquities. The prophecy was fulfilled before that generation passed away. God's wrath literally overtook the Jews when the city of Jerusalem was captured. The temple was destroyed, with almost all of its inhabitants killed or enslaved.

The fall of Jerusalem is the most significant event in the history of Christianity besides the crucifixion of Christ in AD 33. It is considered highly insignificant from the contemporary Christian perspective. However, the destruction of the temple, and the resultant collapse of the ecclesiastical polity of Judaism was a crucial event in the manifestation and elevation of spiritual Israel.[112]

My research on the history of the fall of Jerusalem in AD 70 was mainly dependent upon the primary sources. Two great ancient historians supplied me with all the information necessary. Josephus, the author of *the Wars of the Jews* provided the Jewish perspective of this war, while the Roman historian Tacitus wrote this event from the Roman perspective. I'd like to express my gratitude for their efforts to create accurate historical records for the future generations.

Beginning with the next chapter, I am going to present the fall of Jerusalem in historical context. This topic is among the most important events, yet it is also among the most ignored issues in Christian history. It is vital to realize that the destruction of Jewish temple marked the end of the old covenant. Without knowing this simple, yet vital truth, it is extremely difficult to see the 1st century eschatological perspective.

⌘

4.2. Causes of the Rebellion

Similar to other rebellions, the Jewish rebellion did not burst out suddenly in AD 66. The seed of rebellion was planted from the beginning of the 1ˢᵗ century when the Romans brought the land of Palestine under its jurisdiction. When the land was put under Roman rule, Caesar demanded his share of the tax. Jews were already paying their dues to their local king and temple priests; they did not welcome the Roman taxation and its collaborators, they were met with hatred and contempt. Even the Bible regards those tax collectors in the same rank with sinners, Mark records that many tax collectors and sinners were also sitting with Jesus and his disciples.[113]

Tax was unbearable enough, yet Caesar demanded not only the material share but also a spiritual one. The practice of emperor worship was popular throughout the empire. To the polytheistic Romans, it was better to have many gods – guardians - as many as possible, thus they naturally, without hesitation, accepted their emperor as a god, or a son of god. It may have been a simple sign of allegiance to the Romans. However, the monotheistic Jews could not accept Caesar as a god, since they already had worshipped one true God.

But the Jews were well aware that non-conformity to the emperor worship meant the extinction of their nation. Thus, in accord with their tradition, they offered daily sacrifices for Caesar. When Petronius, a general dispatched by Caius Caesar, demanded the full emperor worship by setting up the emperor's statues in the temple, Jews replied:

"We offer sacrifices twice every day for Caesar, and for the Roman people;" but that if he would place the images among them, he must first sacrifice the whole Jewish nation; and that they were ready to expose themselves, together with their children and wives, to be slain.[114]

Knowing that the Jewish resistance was not from a political cause but from a religious one, Romans remained content with the priests performing daily sacrifices for Caesar. Sacrifices for Caesar continued on until the final revolt began. Temple priests' refusal to sacrifice for Caesar was an indication of the rebellion.

The priests were originally descendants of the tribe of Levi. But since the reign of Herod, the priests were to be appointed by the king Herod, who was also an appointee of Rome. This signified that both Israel's state and religion were under the control of Romans.

In addition to political and religious monopolies, the corrupted Roman governors who succeeded Festus brought social unrest. Albinus was the first among the troubling administrators.

Accordingly, he did not only, in his political capacity, steal and plunder every one's substance, nor did he only burden the whole nation with taxes, but he permitted the relations of such as were in prison for robbery, and had been laid there, either by the senate of every city, or by the former procurators, to redeem them for money; and nobody remained in the prisons as a malefactor but he who gave him nothing.[115]

The successor of Albinus, Florus was more excellent in pursuing the path of his predecessor. He spoiled whole cities, and ruined entire bodies of men at once, and did almost publicly proclaim it all the country over, that they had liberty given them to turn robbers, upon this condition, that he might go shares with them in the spoils. Accordingly, his greediness of gain was the occasion that entire toparchies were brought to desolation; and a great many of the people left their own country, and fled into foreign provinces.[116]

Among them were Essenes who built up monasteries and surrounded their communities with walls. According to Josephus, "They dispense their anger after a just manner, and restrain their passion. They are eminent for fidelity, and are the ministers of peace; whatsoever they say also is firmer than an oath; but swearing is avoided by them, and they esteem it worse than perjury; for they say, that he who cannot be believed without swearing by God, is already condemned. They also take great pains in studying the writings of the ancients, and choose out of them what is most for the advantage of their soul and body; and they inquire after such roots and medicinal stones as may cure their distempers."[117] Despite their effort to maintain peace and justice, their communities were wiped out by the Roman legions led by Titus before the siege upon Jerusalem began. Their towns remained uninhabited for more than nineteen centuries.

In 1947, the Dead Sea scroll was discovered in a Qumran cave near the Essenes community. With the scroll of the Old Testament, there were prophecies concerning the Messiah. Surprisingly, their prophecies did not accord with their peaceful manner of living. According to the Essenes, the world, as they saw it, is divided into two innately hostile camps – the Sons of Light, representing the forces of truth and righteousness, and the Sons of Darkness. Each of these camps is controlled by heavenly beings appointed by God. There is a Prince of Light and an Angel of Darkness, and war continuously rages between these two powers at every level, from the sphere of the angels down to the innermost chambers of the human soul. Every man and woman belongs to one of the two groups, and no one has much choice over which camp he or she is in, for God predestines the enrollments. Even so, the Angel of Darkness keeps trying to ensnare the souls of the righteousness, who must constantly, battle against him.[118]

The struggle is predestined to conclude with the victory of God. On Judgment Day, the Sons of Light will prevail. Not just one messianic figure will appear, but three: a prophet as foretold by Moses, a kingly messiah descended from David, and a priestly messiah, who is the most important of all. At their arrival, the Lord's angelic armies will give forth a great shout, the earth's foundation will shake, "and a war of the mighty ones of the heavens will spread throughout the world." The devastation will be fearsome, consuming all creation, but at its finish a new order will prevail with all evil abolished and "righteousness revealed as the sun." As in the apocalyptic scenarios of other visionaries, the elect will live in eternal peace and happiness, while the wicked will fall to perdition.[119]

As illustrated from Essenes' example, considering themselves as the Sons of Light, and the Romans as the Sons of Darkness, Jews saw such prophecy as a good omen. This prophecy may illustrate the fact that Jews desperately sought for the divine intervention as they were brutally oppressed by the Romans. Standing powerless against the Roman tyranny, Jews waited for the deliverance of Messiah. To them, it seemed evident that the end was near. This apocalyptic hope for the end of Roman rule and the rebirth of Israel was the driving force of future rebellion in AD 66.

⌘

4.3. Unexplainable & Unquestionable Signs

Before the fall of Jerusalem, there were many supernatural signs that foretold the Jews of the future desolation of their land. The validity of these claims remains mysterious, since it is impossible to examine these signs that took place nearly 2,000 years ago. Only the historical records indicate that the supernatural events took place before the fall of Jerusalem in AD 70. Josephus begins his account on the apocalyptic signs by condemning the present – 1st century – generation for their unbelief.

Thus were the miserable people persuaded by these deceivers, and such as belied God himself; while they did not attend, nor give credit, to the signs that were so evident and did so plainly foretell their future desolation; but, like men infatuated, without either eyes to see, or minds to consider, did not regard the denunciations that God made to them.[120]

Various Signs of the Future Desolation

Today we hear many preachers claiming that the present, or future generation will be so unfaithful as to deny God and his visible signs which would take place at the second coming; the situation was similar back in days of Josephus. He mentions several signs that seem implausible when viewed from our modern scientific perspective, some of them are identical to the signs from Tacitus's account.

Thus there was a star resembling a sword, which stood over the city, and a comet, that continued a whole year. Thus also, before the Jews' rebellion, and before those commotions which preceded the war, when the people were come in great crowds to the feast of unleavened bread, on the eighth day of the month Xanthicus [Nisan], and at the ninth hour of the night, so great a light

79

shone round the altar and the holy house, that it appeared to be bright day time; which light lasted for half an hour.[121]

Besides these, a few days after that feast, on the twenty-first day of the month Artemisius [Jyar], a certain prodigious and incredible phenomenon appeared; I suppose the account of it would seem to be a fable, were it not related by those that saw it, and were not the events that followed it of so considerable a nature as to deserve such signals; for, before sunsetting, chariots and troops of soldiers in their armor were seen running about among the clouds, and surrounding of cities. Moreover at that feast which we call Pentecost, as priests were going by night into the inner [court of the] temple, as their custom was, to perform their sacred ministrations, they said that, in the first place, they felt a quaking, and heard a great noise, and after that they heard a sound as of a great multitude, saying, "Let us remove hence."[122]

It is possible that Josephus may have exaggerated the events as to appear them supernatural and mystical. Yet, it is more astonishing to discover that the Roman historian Tacitus also included the similar signs, which Josephus wrote of. Following are excerpts from Tacitus's writing.

Prodigies had occurred, which this nation, prone to superstition, but hating all religious rites, did not deem it lawful to expiate by offering and sacrifice. There had been seen hosts joining battle in the skies, the fiery gleam of arms, the temple illuminated by a sudden radiance from the clouds. The doors of the inner shrine were suddenly thrown open, and a voice of more than mortal tone was heard to cry that the Gods were departing. At the same instant there was a mighty stir as of departure. Some few put a fearful meaning on these events, but in most there was a firm persuasion, that in the ancient records of their priests was contained a prediction of how at this very time the East was to grow powerful, and rulers, coming from Judæa, were to acquire universal empire.[123]

Although these two historians, Josephus and Tacitus, had different perspectives, they nevertheless had similar accounts concerning the signs that preceded the fall of Jerusalem. Below is another mysterious event that Josephus recorded.

Woe, Woe to Jerusalem!

*But, what is still more terrible there was one Jesus, the son of Ananus, a plebeian and a husbandman, who, four years before the war began, and at a time when the city was in very great peace and prosperity, came to that feast whereon it is our custom for everyone to make tabernacles to God in the temple, began on a sudden cry aloud, "**A voice from the east, a voice from the west, a voice from the four winds, a voice against Jerusalem and the holy house, a voice against the bridegrooms and the brides, and a voice against this whole people!**" This was his cry, as he went about by day and by night, in all the lanes of the city. However, certain of the most eminent among the populace had great indignation at this dire cry of his, and took up the man, and gave him a great number of severe stripes; yet did not he either say anything for himself, or anything peculiar to those that chastised him, but still he went on with the same words which he cried before. Hereupon our rulers supposing, as the case proved to be, that this was a sort of divine fury in the man, brought him to the Roman procurator; where he was whipped till his bones were laid bare; yet did he not make any supplication for himself, nor shed any tears, but turning his voice to the most lamentable tone possible, at every stroke of the whip his answer was, "**Woe, woe to Jerusalem!**" And when Albinus (for he was then our procurator) asked him who he was, and whence he came, and why he uttered such words; he made no manner of reply to what he said, but still did not leave off his melancholy ditty, till Albinus took him to be a madman, and dismissed him. Now, during all the time that passed before the war began, this man did not go near any of the citizens, nor was seen by them while he said so; but he every day uttered these lamentable words, as if it were his premeditated vow, "**Woe, woe to Jerusalem!**" Nor did he give ill words to any of those that beat him every day, nor good words to those that gave him food; but this was his reply to all men, and indeed no other than a melancholy presage of what was to come. This cry of his was the loudest at the festivals; and he continued this ditty for seven years and five months, without growing hoarse, or being tired therewith, until the very time that he saw his presage in earnest fulfilled in our siege, when it ceased; for as he was going round upon the wall, he cried out with his utmost force, "**Woe, woe, to the city again, and to the people, and to the holy house!**" And just as he added at the last,*

- *"**Woe, woe, to myself also!**" there came a stone out of one of the engines, and smote him, and killed him immediately; and as he was uttering the very same presages, he gave up the ghost.*[124]

Great Fire in Rome

For the 1st century Christians, nothing seemed to be more evident sign of the apocalypse than Nero's persecution of Christians, which included the crucifixion of Peter and execution of Paul. Nero started persecuting Christians when he set off great fire in Rome, which burned down a large portion of the city; he used Christians as scapegoats. Tacitus describes its enormous damage to the city. He doesn't know the exact cause of this fire, but he mentions the possibility of Nero being involved with this incident.

A disaster followed, whether accidental or treacherously contrived by the emperor, is uncertain, as authors have given both accounts, worse, however, and more dreadful than any which have ever happened to this city by the violence of fire. It had its beginning in that part of the circus which adjoins the Palatine and Cælian hills, where, amid the shops containing inflammable wares, the conflagration both broke out and instantly became so fierce and so rapid from the wind that it seized in its grasp the entire length of the circus. For here there were no houses fenced in by solid masonry, or temples surrounded by walls, or any other obstacle to interpose delay. The blaze in its fury ran first through the level portion of the city, then rising to the hills, while it again devastated every place below them...[125]

Nero blamed Christians for the disaster and started his persecution. Christians were perfect targets; due to the distorted perceptions that Romans held, Christians were seen with suspicion and hatred.

*But all human efforts, all the lavish gifts of the emperor, and the propitiations of the gods, did not banish the sinister belief that the conflagration was the result of an order. Consequently, to get rid of the report, **Nero fastened the guilt and inflicted the most exquisite tortures on a class hated for their abominations, called Christians by the populace.** Christus, from whom the name had its origin, suffered the extreme penalty during the reign*

*of Tiberius at the hands of one of our procurators, Pontius Pilatus,
and a most mischievous superstition, thus checked for the moment,
again broke out not only in Judæa, the first source of the evil, but
even in Rome, where all things hideous and shameful from every
part of the world find their centre and become popular. Accordingly, an arrest was first made of all who pleaded guilty; then, upon
their information, **an immense multitude was convicted, not
so much of the crime of firing the city, as of hatred against
mankind.** Mockery of every sort was added to their deaths. Covered with the skins of beasts, they were torn by dogs and perished,
or were nailed to crosses, or were doomed to the flames and burnt,
to sere as a nightly illumination, when daylight had expired.[126]*

Above excerpt clearly illustrates the Roman view of
Christians. They were regarded similar to how we view modern
day's extreme cults, or of the sort. Yet, even from Roman perspective, the persecution was far severe. Rome was known
for its cultural - including religion – tolerance on its subjects,
yet they showed extreme hostility toward Christians. Why
would Romans convict Christians of "hatred against mankind"? There must have been a great cultural misunderstand-
ing.

One brilliant job that Nero performed – which other
emperors could not – in his persecution was that he was able to
distinguish the differences between Jews and Christians. Generally, Christians were treated as one variation of the Jews.
Truly, they held a lot in common.

The early church struggled over the issue whether they
were to retain their Jewish aspects or to establish themselves as
global religion of the empire, which meant a separation from
the old covenant Judaism. Nevertheless, both Jews and Christians believed that the end of this world was approaching. All
the visible signs and events that preceded the fall of Jerusalem
served as warnings of the future apocalypse. It was the event
that was finally going to determine the fates of today's two great
religions, Christianity and Judaism.

⌘

4.4. Jewish War

The rebellion of 66 AD would not have occurred if the Roman administration had been more deliberate. The Roman governor Florus was the one who attempted to make a war with the Jews, so that he would be able to plunder the treasures in the holy temple. His tyranny had humiliated priests and teachers of the law, the spiritual heads of Israel, far too offensively. Florus simply expected to have a short-term conflict, which would simply buy him an opportunity to capture the temple. What he did not understand was the Jewish determination for independence aided by the interpretations of ancient prophecies, and Jerusalem's geographical advantage. In three directions, valleys surrounded this heavily fortified city. Also, their strong sense of pride as a nation chosen by God also served as a stimulant in this revolt.

Refusal of Daily Sacrifice for Caesar

Temple priests refusing to sacrifice for Caesar and Rome, was a declaration of war, or at least that is how the Romans saw it. The administration of Florus had worsened the situation in Judea. Jews could not stand being ruled by foreigners whom they considered inferior. Although it was considered a national suicide to go to war with the Romans, the humiliations that Israel suffered were far too great.

At the same time Eleazar, the sons of Ananias the high priest, a very bold youth, who was at that time governor of the temple, persuaded those that officiated in the divine service to receive no gift or sacrifice for any foreigner. And this was the true beginning of our war with the Romans; for they rejected the sacrifice of Caesar on this account... [127]

Sicarii's siege of Masada

The rebellion finally began. Some excited Jews seized the fort Masada, which was garrisoned by the Roman guards. After slaying the Romans there, Jews put their men to keep it.

Sicarii was the name for the robbers who carried daggers called "Sicae". Its head was a man named Manahem. He "took some of the men of note with him, and retired to Masada, where he broke open king Herod's armory, and gave arms not only to his own people, but to other robbers also. These he made use of for a guard, and returned in the state of a king to Jerusalem; he became the leader of the sedition, and gave orders for continuing the siege"[128].

Manahem's Fate

Unlike other heads of the rebellion, Manahem was a lower classman. Priests could not stand a former robber ruling their nation as a king. His tyranny persuaded the multitude to take sides with Eleazar and the temple priests.

> ...they made an assault upon him in the temple; for he went up thither to worship in a pompous manner, and adorned with royal garments, and had his followers with him in their armor. But Eleazar and his party fell violently upon him, as did also the rest of the people, and taking up stones to attack him withal, they threw them at the sohister, and thought that if he were once ruined, the entire sedition would fall to the ground. Now Manahem and his party made resistance for a while; but when they perceived that the whole multitude were falling upon them, they fled which was every one was able; those that were caught were slain, and those that hid themselves were searched for. A few there were of them who privately escaped to Masada, among whom was Eleazar, the son of Jarius, who was of kin to Manahem, and acted the part of a tyrant at Masada afterward. As for Manahem himself, he ran away to the place called Ophla, and there lay skulking in private; but they took him alive, and drew him out before them all; they then tortured him with many sorts of torments, and after all slew him...[129]

With its head slain, Sicarii forces retreat to the fort Masada, and remains there during the entire rebellion. After

4. The Fall of Jerusalem

Jerusalem falls, Titus leads his army to siege Masada. Strangely, during 7 years Sicarii doesn't make a single move against the Romans, or to other Zealot armies. Eventually, the fort is captured and its inhabitants end up in mass suicide.

Nero orders Vespasian to subdue the Rebellion

To Nero, a revolt in the land of Palestine was an excellent opportunity to draw the general public's discontent abroad. His reign quickly exhausted the Roman treasury and now he had to plunder the riches of the East to sustain his imperial throne.

So Nero esteemed these circumstances as favorable omens, and saw that Vespasian's age gave him sure experience, and great skill, and that he had his sons as hostages for his fidelity to himself, and that the flourishing age they were in would make them fit instruments under their father's prudence. Perhaps also there was some interposition of Providence, which was paving the way for Vespasian's being himself emperor afterwards.[130]

Upon the whole he sent this man to take upon him the command of the armies that were in Syria; but this not without great encomiums and flattering compellations, such as necessity required, and such as might mollify him into complaisance. So Vespasian sent his son Titus from Achaia, where he had been with Nero, to Alexandria, to bring back with him from thence the fifth and tenth legions, while he himself, when he had passed over the Hellespont, came by land into Syria, where he gathered together, the Roman forces, with a considerable number of auxiliaries from the kings in that neighborhood.[131]

Arriving from north, Vespasian plundered the Galilean countryside. Many Jews fled to Jotapata, which Josephus fortified. Josephus recorded: "By this means he provoked the Romans to treat the country according to the law of war: nor did the Romans, out of the anger they bore at this attempt, leave off either by night or by day, burning the places in the plain, or stealing away the cattle that were in the country, and killing whatsoever appeared capable of fighting perpetually, and leading the weaker people as slaves into captivity: so that Galilee was all over filled with fire and blood; nor was it exempted from any kind of misery or calamity; for the only refuge they had was this, that when they were pursued, they could retire to the cities which had wall built them by Josephus."[132]

The Siege of Jotapata

With all the inhabitants of Galilee fleeing to Jotapata, it became necessary for Vespasian to capture the fort before advancing toward Jerusalem. He expected a short battle, but it was a long fought siege. Jews put up great resistance, which the Romans did not expect to encounter. Yet the situation grew worse for the Jews as days passed. Josephus describes in the greatest detail, since he was the commander of the defenders.

> *The noise of the instruments themselves was very terrible, the sound of the darts and stones that were thrown by them was so also; of the same sort was that noise the dead bodies made, when they were dashed against the wall; and indeed dreadful was the clamor which these things raised in the women within the city, which was echoed back at the same time by the cries of such as were slain; while the whole space of ground whereon they fought ran with blood, and the wall might have been ascended over by the bodies of the dead carcasses; the mountains also contributed to increase the noise by their echoes; nor was there on that night anything of terror wanting that could either affect the hearing or the sight: yet did a great part of those that fought so hard for Jotapata fall manfully, as were a great part of them wounded.*[133]

After both sides inflicted mass casualties to each other, the Romans finally overwhelmed the Jews. Josephus safely escaped the battle, and was later captured. Vespasian had conquered Galilee.

> *And on this day the Romans slew all the multitude that appeared openly; but on the following days they searched the hiding places, and fell upon those that were underground, and in the caverns, and went thus through every age, excepting the infants and the women, and of these there were gathered together as captives twelve hundred; and as for those that were slain at the taking of the city, and in the former fights, they were numbered to be forty thousand. So Vespasian gave order that the city should be entirely demolished, and all the fortifications burnt down. And thus was*

4. The Fall of Jerusalem

Jotapata taken, in the thirteenth year of the reign of Nero, on the first day of the month Panemus [Tamuz].[134]

Death of Nero (68 AD)

In 68 AD, the emperor Nero was killed and a civil war erupted. After Nero's death, his generals competed for the throne. Vespasian saw this incident as a perfect chance to take the empire by force. He thus abandoned the campaign in Palestine and advanced toward Rome. With the support of his army, he overtook the government and crowned himself as Caesar. He did not return to Palestine; he handed over the campaign to his son Titus. Suppressing the revolt in Palestine was an opportunity for Flavians to demonstrate that they were worthy of the imperial throne.

Civil War in Jerusalem

While Vespasian left Palestine, Jews were not concerned with preparing for future Roman invasion. They divided themselves up into several factions; these factions struggled for dominance. Their armies surrounded the city and raided each other. Josephus mentions the seditious factions that fought over the city.

…it so happened that the sedition at Jerusalem was revived, and parted into three factions, and that one faction fought against the other; which partition in such evil cases may be said to be a good thing, and the effect of divine justice. Now as to the attack the zealots made upon the people, and which I esteem the beginning of the city's destruction, it hath been already explained after an accurate manner; as also whence it arose, and to how great a mischief it was increased; but for the present sedition, one should not mistake if he called it a sedition begotten by another sedition, and to be like a wild beast grown mad, which for want of food from abroad, fell now upon eating its own flesh.[135]

Unity among the people would not have saved them from the Roman armies. The situation was against their favor. Their strong sense of unity faded away. Factional conflicts dominated the everyday life. Concerning these seditious fac-

89

tions, Josephus gives us detailed account.

> *And now there were three treacherous factions in the city, the one parted from the other. Eleazar and his party, that kept the sacred firstfruits, came against John in their cups. Those that were with John plundered the populace, and went out with zeal against Simon. This Simon had his supply of provisions from the city, in oppositions to the seditious. When, therefore, John was assaulted on both sides, he made his men turn about, throwing his darts upon those citizens that came up against him, from the cloisters he had in his possession, while he opposed those that attacked him from the temple by his engines of war; and if at any time he was freed from those that were above him, which happened frequently, from their being drunk and tired, he sallied out with a great number upon Simon and his party; and this he did always in such parts of the city as he could come at, till he set on fire those houses that were full of corn, and of all other provisions. The same thing was done by Simon, when, upon the other's retreat, he attacked the city also; as if they had, on purpose, done it to serve the Romans, by destroying what the city had laid up against the siege, and by thus cutting off the nerves of their own power.[136]*

Blood Feast in the Holy House

Jerusalem lost its peace and prosperity. Things that rebels committed before its siege indicated that the end was near. Even the holy temple could not escape the consequences of sedition. God no longer dwelt in Israel, which was about to pass away.

> *…for those darts that were thrown by the engines came with that force, that they went all over the buildings, and reached as far as the altar, and the temple itself, and fell upon the priests, and those (the Levites) that were about the sacred offices; insomuch that in any persons who came thither with great zeal from the ends of the earth, to offer sacrifices at this celebrated place, which was esteemed holy by all mankind, fell down before their own sacrifices themselves, and sprinkled that altar which was venerable among all men, both Greeks and Barbarians, with their own blood; till the dead bodies of strangers were mingled together with those of their own country, and those of profane persons with those of the priests, and the blood of all sorts of dead carcasses stood in lakes in*

the holy courts themselves.[137]

Thus, the holy house itself was corrupted with the murders that took place within it. No longer was the old covenant temple fit to be God's dwelling place. Even Josephus cried, "O most wretched city, what misery so great as this didst thou suffer from the Romans, when they came to purify thee from they intestine hatred! For thou couldst be no longer a place fit for God, nor couldst thou longer continue in being, after thou hadst been a sepulchre for the bodies of thine own people, and hadst made the holy house itself a burying-place in this civil war of thine! Yet mayest thou again grow better, if perchance thou wilt hereafter appease the anger of that God who is the author of thy destruction."[138]

Witnessing these terrible miseries, also remembering what Jesus foretold, **"When you see Jerusalem being surrounded by armies, you will know that its desolation is near. Then let those in Judea flee to the mountains, let those in the city get out, and let those in the country not enter the city. For this is the time in fulfillment of all that has been written"**[139], Christians left the city knowing that the apocalypse was approaching. Among the million Jews slaughtered, there is not a single record concerning Christians being killed in the siege. They did what Jesus told them; they lived.

Titus returns to Jerusalem

Vespasian gave his son Titus control of the legions of the East, which were deployed against the Jewish forces in Palestine. Tacitus provides us his account concerning the turning point of conquest in Judea.

Early in this year Titus Cæsar, who had been selected by his father to complete the subjugation of Judæa, and who had gained distinction as a soldier while both were still subjects, began to rise in power and reputation, as armies and provinces emulated each other in their attachment to him. The young man himself, anxious to be thought superior to his station, was ever displaying his gracefulness and his energy in war. By his courtesy and affability he called forth a willing obedience, and he often mixed with the common soldiers, while working or marching, without impairing his dignity as general. He found in Judæa three legions, the 5th, the

10th, and the 15th, all old troops of Vespasian's. To these he added the 12th from Syria, and some men belonging to the 18th and 3rd, whom he had withdrawn from Alexandria. This force was accompanied by twenty cohorts of allied troops and eight squadrons of cavalry, by the two kings Agrippa and Sohemus, by the auxiliary forces of king Antiochus, by a strong contingent of Arabs, who hated the Jews with the usual hatred of neighbours, and, lastly, by many persons brought from the capital and from Italy by private hopes of securing the yet unengaged affections of the Prince. With this force Titus entered the enemy's territory, preserving strict order on his march, reconnoitring every spot, and always ready to give battle. At last he encamped near Jerusalem.[140]

The Romans were well aware of the fact that Jews were occupied with the factional conflicts before they arrived. As Romans conquered the countryside, more Jews entered Jerusalem. Tacitus recorded:

Their numbers were increased by a vast rabble collected from the overthrow of the other cities. All the most obstinate rebels had escaped into the place, and perpetual seditions were the consequence. There were three generals, and as many armies. Simon held the outer and larger circuit of walls. John, also called Bargioras, occupied the middle city. Eleazar had fortified the temple. John and Simon were strong in numbers and equipment, Eleazar in position. There were continual skirmishes, surprises, and incendiary fires, and a vast quantity of corn was burnt. Before long John sent some emissaries, who, under pretence of sacrificing, slaughtered Eleazar and his partisans, and gained possession of the temple. The city was thus divided between two factions, till, as the Romans approached, war with the foreigner brought about a reconciliation.[141]

Titus entered the scene. Jewish factions were forced to end their conflicts and fight against their common enemy, the Romans. Although Jews had been wasting time fighting amongst themselves, they still had their strongly fortified city. They also gained combat experience from the factional conflicts. What they lacked was a strong leader, who could unite both factions. John and Simon cooperated to a certain degree, but they were not fit to lead Israel out of the calamity that she was going to encounter. It was a tragedy for the 1st century Jews that Moses did not live anymore among them to lead them out of their destructive fate.

Famine within the City

Despite the lack of a strong leader, Jews possessed a strong fortification with geographical advantage. Their manpower was far greater than that of the Romans. Relying on the wall granted Jews safety from the Roman army, but as siege continued, Jews had to face the problems within the walls. The situation of Jerusalem was becoming worse.

> *The madness of the seditious did also increase together with their famine, and both those miseries were every day inflamed more and more; for there was no corn which anywhere appeared publicly, but the robbers came running into, and searched men's private houses; and then, if they found any, they tormented them, because they had denied they had any; and if they found none, they tormented them worse, because they supposed they had more carefully concealed it.*[142]
>
> *It was now a miserable case, and a sight that would justly bring tears into our eyes, how men stood as to their food, while the more powerful had more than enough, and the weaker were lamenting (for want of it). But the famine was too hard for all other passions, and it is destructive to nothing so much as to modesty; for what was otherwise worthy of reverence was in this case despised; insomuch that children pulled the very morsels that their fathers were eating out of their very mouths, and, what was still more to be pitied, so did the mothers do as to their infants; and when those that were most dear were perishing under their hands, they were not ashamed to take from them the very last drops that might preserve their lives...*[143]

Simon and John; the Leaders of Sedition

Famine was one problem that Jews had to deal with. The tyrants forced the situation worse. Tyrants and their henchmen plundered their countrymen more than the Romans could ever have. Josephus recorded:

> *Now the warlike men that were in the city, and the mul-*

titude of the seditious that were with Simon, were ten thousand, besides the Idumeans. Those ten thousand had fifty commanders, over whom this Simon was supreme. The Idumeans that paid him homage were five thousand, and had eight commanders, among whom those of greatest fame were Jacob the son of Sosas, and Simon, the son of Cathlas. John, who had seized upon the temple, had six thousand armed men, under twenty commanders; the zealots also that had come to him, and left off their opposition, were two thousand four hundred, and had the same commander that they had formerly, Eleazar, together with Simon the son of Arinus.[144]

These factions lost their sense of unity as they were gradually made comfortable with the present condition of Romans surrounding their city.

But although they had grown wiser at the first onset the Romans made upon them, this lasted but a while; for they returned to their former madness, and separated one from another; and fought it out, and did everything that the besiegers could desire them to do; for they never suffered anything that was worse from the Romans than they made each other suffer...[145]

Some Jews were wise to realize the grave danger that they were facing. They knew that their country needed all the possible resources and manpower to repel the Romans, but the zealots were spending their precious time fighting against their countrymen. Resentful toward these seditions, but powerless over the course of his nation, a high priest Ananus spoke with a flood of tears in his eyes. "Certainly, it had been good for me to die before I had seen the house of God full of so many abominations, or these sacred places that ought not to be trodden upon at random, filled with the feet of these blood-shedding villains; yet do I, who am clothed with the vestments of the high priesthood, and am called by that most venerable name [of high priest], still live, and am but too fond of living, and cannot endure to undergo a death which would be the glory of my old age..."[146]

After Ananus's speech, a great multitude gathered to defy the zealots. However, the followers of Ananus were practically unarmed and inexperienced with combat, while the zealots used their arms almost daily. Yet, there were so many people following Ananus that the seditions could not take much action in resisting the multitude.

The tyrant John pretended as if he sided with Ananus. According to Josephus, "He was a man of great craft, and bore about him in his soul strong passion after tyranny, and at a distance was the adviser in these actions; and indeed at this time he pretended to be of the people's opinion, and went all about with Ananus when he consulted the great men every day, and in the nighttime also when he went around the watch; but he divulged their secrets to the zealots; and everything that the people deliberated about was by his means known to their enemies"[147].

John plotted with the zealots to attack the temple with the Idumeans, whom Simon controlled. Although the multitude had a larger number than the zealots, many were old men and women. The majority of young men were zealots. After hours of plundering, the outer temple overflowed with blood, eight thousand five hundred laid dead. The high priests, Ananus and Jesus were slain. Josephus considers Ananus's death as "the beginning of the destruction of the city". Jerusalem lost its spiritual head. Many priests were slain that day. From this point on, Simon and John were truly the rulers of Judean state.

Jesus warned his followers of the "abomination of desolation"[148] that would stand in the holy place. His prophecy was being fulfilled through the conflicts in Jerusalem before AD 70, the end was approaching near.

Tyranny

After the death of Ananus and the massacre of his multitude, the powers of two tyrants went unchecked. Jews suffered greatly under these men. They were stripped off of their basic rights. According to Josephus: "These were the afflictions which the lower sort of people suffered from these tyrants' guards; but for the men that were in dignity, and withal were rich, they were carried before they tyrants themselves; some of whom were falsely accused of laying treacherous plots, and so were destroyed; others of them were charged with designs of betraying the city to the Romans: but the readiest way of all was this, to suborn somebody to affirm that they were resolved to desert the enemy; and he who was utterly despoiled of what he had by Simon, was sent back again to John, as of those who had been already plundered by John, Simon got what remained, insomuch that they drank the blood of populace to one another, and divided the dead bodies of the poor creatures between them"[149].

Concerning the man of lawlessness - that Paul mentioned in his second letter to Thessalonians; it is probable that this man is either John, Simon, or even Manahem. They both were lawless as to disrespect the law and murder the priests, thereby profaning the holy temple. These two lawless men will be discussed in later part of the chapter.

The Miseries of Jerusalem

As the siege started, this rebellion proved to be the cause of unprecedented miseries. Jews inflicted pain toward each other more than any foreigners could have done to them. Josephus said:

It is therefore impossible to go distinctly over every instance of these men's iniquity. I shall therefore speak my mind here at once briefly: - That neither did any other city ever suffer such miseries, nor did any age ever breed a generation more fruitful in wickedness that this was, from the beginning of the world.[150]

The Son Cometh

This topic is one of the most mysterious events - in significance – that I was interested in while studying the rebellion. It would probably be related in some way with Christ's Parousia, the coming of the Son. During the siege, Roman engines threw darts and stones over the wall.

Now, the stones that were cast were of the weight of a talent, and were carried two furlongs and farther. The blow they gave was no way to be sustained, not only by those that stood first in the way, but by those that were beyond them for a great space. As for the Jews, they at first watched the coming of the stone, for it was of a white color, and could therefore not only be perceived by the great noise it made, but could be seen also before it came by its brightness; accordingly the watchmen that sat upon the towers gave them notice when the engine was let go, and the stone came from it, and cried out aloud in their own country language, "THE SON COMETH:"[151]

Why did this man say "the Son cometh?" Is it a mistranslation, or is there actually a significance behind this fact? Here's the translator's note

What should be the meaning of this signal or watchword, when the watchman saw a stone coming from the engine, "The Son Cometh," or what mistake there is in the reading, I cannot tell. The MSS. Both Greek and Latin, all agree in this reading: and I cannot approve of any groundless conjectural alteration of the text from *huios* to *ios*, that not the *son* or a *stone*, but that the *arrow* or *dart* cometh; as hath been made by Dr. Hudson, and not corrected by Havercamp. Had Josephus written even his first edition of these books of the *War* in pure Hebrew at Jerusalem, the Hebrew word for a son is so like that for a stone, *ben* and *eben*, that such a correction might have been more easily admitted. But Josephus wrote his former edition for the use of the Jews beyond Euphrates, and so in the Chaldee language, as he did this second edition in the Greek language; and *bar* was the Chaldee word for *son*, instead of the Hebrew *ben*, and was used, not only in Chaldea, etc., but in Judea also, as the New Testament informs us: Dio also lets us know, that the very Romans at Rome pronounced the name of Simon the son of Gioras, *Bar Poras* for *Bar Gioras*, as we learn from Xiphiline, p.217. Roland takes notice, "that many will here look for a mystery, as though the meaning were, that the Son of God came now to take vengeance on the sins of the Jewish nation;" which is indeed the truth of the fact, but hardly what the Jews could now mean: unless possibly by way of derision of Christ's threatening so often that he would come at the head of the Roman army for their destruction. But even this interpretation has but a very small degree of probability. If I were to make an emendation by mere conjecture, I would read *petros* instead of *huios*, though the likeness be not so great as in *ios*; because that is the word used by Josephus just before, as has been already noted on this very occasion, while *ios*, an arrow or dart, is only a poetical word, and never used by Josephus elsewhere, and is indeed no way suitable to the occasion, this engine not throwing arrows or darts, but great stones, at this time.[152]

The actual text says "The Son Cometh". Why would the translators, historians and theologians attempt to change the original text? Thankfully, Whiston did not change the text, which gives us an opportunity to look at the unbiased translation of Josephus's writing. Same thing happened with the making of NIV Bible and the translators changed the text. The reason why they are untruthful to themselves is because their map – perspective does not fit with the historical records in original context. The Son coming in AD 70 may seem highly implausible from their traditional perspective. But the historical references – including the Bible, tells us of the Parousia's fulfillment in AD 70.

Mass Crucifixion

To quickly dismiss the Jewish resistance, Titus decided to prey upon their fear. His army caught the Jews who were fleeing from the city. In encountering Romans, Jews feared that they would be punished, thus they resisted. Their resistance angered the Romans even worse, and the ones who fought against the Romans were tortured to death. According to Josephus, "…they were first whipped, and then tormented with all sorts of tortures before they died, and were then crucified before the wall of the city…(abridged) So the soldiers out of the wrath and hatred they bore the Jews, nailed those they caught, one after one way, another after another, to the crosses, by way of jest; when their multitude was so great, that room was wanting for the crosses, and crosses wanting for the bodies."[153] In one day, as many as 500 hundred Jews were crucified.

The Romans crucified those Jews to weaken the Jewish resistance. But the seditions made the populace believe firmly that the Romans were going to crucify them anyway if they left the city. Titus's plan did not work successfully, and as a result more Jews were sacrificed.

Famine and Calamity

So all hope of escaping was not cut off from the Jews, together with their liberty of going out of the city. Then did the famine widen its progress, and devoured the people by whole houses and families; the upper rooms were full of women and children that were dying by famine; and the lanes of the city were full of the dead bodies of the aged; the children also and the young men wandered about the marketplaces like shadows, all swelled with the famine, and fell down dead wheresoever their misery seized them. As for burying them, those that were sick themselves were not able to do it; and those that were hearty and well were deterred from doing it by the great multitude of those dead bodies, and by the uncertainty there was how soon they should die themselves, for many died as they were burying others, and many went to their coffins before that fatal hour was come![154]

The famine slowly took over the populace and now was moving toward the seditions that caused all the miseries. Jews were being weakened from the inside and now very few remained to defend the city against the Romans.

The Great Slaughters and Sacrilege that were in Jerusalem

Jesus once said that the fall of Jerusalem was going to be an event, which would be "unequaled from the beginning of the world until now – and never to be equaled again."[155] Many prophecy students claim, citing this verse, that the fall of Jerusalem was just a minor local conflict in the Roman Empire. Is there really a degree or a standard of measurement for calamities and miseries? Few Christians study about the fall of Jerusalem; the majority simply regards it as an event when the temple fell.

To let the readers feel the extremity of brutality, fear and danger that are associated with the siege of Jerusalem, I prepared to illustrate the account of Josephus concerning the detailed scenes of the fall of Jerusalem.

Roman army that surrounded the city was a highly organized professional armed force. However, the Horde of Israel's neighboring nations had little control over their men. As Josephus recorded, their basic interest was to plunder the Jews so they could profit.

One of the most disgusting and brutal murders were carried out by these Arabian and Syrian neighbors. Josephus recorded:

...there was found among the Syrian deserters a certain person who was caught gathering pieces of gold out of the excre-

ments of the Jews' bellies; for the deserters used to swallow such pieces of gold, as we told you before, when they came out; and for these did the seditious search them all; for there was a great quantity of gold in the city, insomuch that as much was now sold [in the Roman camp] for twelve Attic [drams], as was sold before for twenty-five; but when this contrivance was discovered in one instance, the fame of it filled their several camps, that the deserters came to them full of gold. So the multitude of the Arabians, with the Syrians, cut up those that came as supplicants, and searched their bellies. Nor does it seem to me that any misery befell the Jews that was more terrible than this, since in one night's time about two thousand of these deserters were thus dissected.[156]

Dissecting bellies for gold is horrible enough. An event that literally signaled the end – of the old covenant – approaching took place in the holy temple. The seditions exploited other people to satisfy their greed. When the populace was drained of all resources, John decided to sack the temple itself. Jesus mentioned the desolating sacrilege in the temple. Such things happening to the temple, surely the end of old covenant was drawing near.

But as for John, when he could no longer plunder the people, he betook himself to sacrilege, and melted down many of the sacred utensils, which had been given to the temple; as also many of those vessels which were necessary for such as ministered about holy things, the caldrons, the dishes, and the tables; nay, he did not abstain from those pouring-vessels that were sent them by Augustus and his wife; for the Roman emperors did ever both honor and adorn this temple; whereas this man, who was a Jew, seized upon what were the donations of foreigners; and said to those that were with him, that it was proper for them to use divine things while they were fighting for the Divinity, without fear, and that such whose warfare is for the temple, should live of the temple, on which account he emptied the vessels of that sacred wine and oil...[157]

The holy house lost its function as a dwelling place of God. Already profaned with murders and despoliation, the temple could no longer serve its original purpose. Without the temple, the old covenant could not exist. These events that took place in the temple signified that there wasn't much time left till its destruction. The revenge for the martyred was about to be complete, but the grand finale was yet to come.

Conflagration upon the Holy House

To the Jews, the temple in Jerusalem was a symbol of their identity and glory. It was a gigantic structure, yet fascinating in its appearance. Many considered it a great wonder of its time.

By the time Titus and his army penetrated the two walls, and confronted the fortified temple, he had to make a choice whether to destroy it or preserve it. Some of his generals believed that the rebellion would not cease as long as the temple stood. Others insisted that the temple be a display of Roman conquest over Judea. Others wanted to let the Jews decide: if the Jews use the temple as a citadel, then the army would burn it. But Titus said "although the Jews should get upon that holy house, and fight us thence, yet ought we not to revenge ourselves on things that are inanimate, instead of the men themselves"[158].

Thus, it was decided that they preserve the temple even if the Jews used it as their last defense. However, desolation was the only fate of the holy house. Josephus recorded: "…as for that house, God had for certain long ago doomed it to the fire; and now that fatal day was come, according to the revolution of ages; it was the tenth day of the month Lous[Ab], upon which it was formerly burnt by the king of Babylon"[159]. A common soldier, out of divine fury according to Josephus, set a fire upon the golden window, which spread out over the entire temple. On the course of temple's conflagration, many were slain, beaten, and had their throats cut wherever they were caught. Dead bodies heaped up in the altar, and a great quantity of blood ran on the floor of the altar.

Josephus regards this event as where "the blood was larger in quantity than the fire, and those that were slain more in number than those that slew them; for the ground did nowhere appear visible". The Romans judged that it was too late to save the temple from its conflagration, thus they set fire on the remaining parts, thereby bringing the temple to its total destruction.

Meanwhile, in this catastrophe, a false prophet proclaimed that they were to get up upon the temple and receive God's signs of their deliverance. This was the last apocalyptic

101

hope that the Jews held. Even at the climax of the siege, Jews thought that God would intervene and save them from this calamity. There was more than one false prophet who seduced the multitude, they were all killed in the siege.

Bringing of Roman ensigns to the Temple

Finally, after the temple's destruction, the Roman armies carried their ensigns to the temple site, the object of their worship. The translator noted: "This (says he) is a remarkable place; and Tertullian truly says in his Apologetic, 16.162, that the entire religion of the Roman camp almost consisted in worshipping the ensigns, in swearing by the ensigns, and in preferring the ensigns before all the [other] gods."[160] The objects of pagan worship, taking over the temple site seems somehow significant as far as the prophetic fulfillment is concerned. Josephus noted:

> And now the Romans, upon the flight of the seditious into the city, and upon the burning of the holy house itself, and of all the buildings round about it, brought their ensigns to the temple, and set them over against its eastern gate; and there did they offer sacrifices to them, and there did they make Titus imperator, with the greatest acclamations of joy.[161]

For seventy years, Romans tried to enforce their pagan worship to the Jews and to practice it in the temple. Titus being the future emperor of Rome, the emperor worship was finally fulfilled through this event. This may not be the identical pagan worship that Paul mentioned in 2 Thessalonians 2:4 – which may have been fulfilled through John, Simon or Manahem, but it nevertheless holds a significance of old covenant's demise. A temple had become gods' dwelling place but God's.

As results of rebellion, Jews lost their priesthood, land, temple, covenant and their personal liberty. As our contemporary preachers usually say, "this is it", this was it for the old covenant. The apocalypse was finally consummated through the temple's conflagration.

4. The Fall of Jerusalem

After 70 AD
Jerusalem fell in 70 AD. It had been four years since the beginning of rebellion, which started with temple priests refusing to sacrifice for Caesar. Now the temple was gone, and so did the Jewish nation. Four years ago, Jerusalem was among the flourished metropolis of its time. From 70 AD and onward, the land became desolate. The entire city was destroyed, including its once mighty fortification. "To conclude, when he (Titus) entirely demolished the rest of the city, and overthrew its walls, he left these towers as a monument of his good fortune"[162].

The city's inhabitants were slain, enslaved, or relocated. The seditious robbers were slain, tall and young men were reserved for displays when he return to Rome in triumph, and the rest of multitude were put into bonds, and were sent to Egyptian mines and other provinces as slaves. A translator noted: "See the several predictions that the Jews, if they became obstinate in their idolatry and wickedness, should be sent again, or sold into Egypt, for their punishment, Deut. 28:68; Jer. 44:7; Hos. 8:13; 9:3; 11:35; 2 Esd. 15:10-14, with Authentic Records, part. 1.49,121, and Reland Palaestina, tom. 2.715."[163]

John and Simon, the tyrants of seditions, suffered same tragedies as others whom they inflicted pain upon. Josephus noted:

…yet did God avenge himself upon them both, in a manner agreeable to justice. As for John, he wanted food, together with his brethren, in these caverns, and begged that the Romans would now give him their right hand for his security, which he had often proudly rejected before; but for Simon, he struggled hard with the distress he was in, till he was forced to surrender himself, as we shall relate hereafter; so he was reserved for triumph, and to be then slain: as was John condemned to perpetual imprisonment[164].

After the rebellion was subdued, there were few minor resistances around the countryside. One of the most famous siege that took place after 70 AD would be the siege of Masada which was completed in 73 AD.

As mentioned in the early part of this chapter, after Manahem's death, Sicarii forces remained in the fort Masada,

103

remaining there completely inactive. When the Romans came, they all committed mass suicide – supposedly. Josephus records that few women and children survived to testify for the things that took place up on the fort, but some scholars believe that the record is inaccurate, that Josephus created the story so that Israel would have a glorious end. Another sedition took place in Cyrene. The remnants of Sicarii and its leader Jonathan stirred up the multitude. However, that was subdued with ease. Jonathan was tormented and burnt alive. Peace returned to the empire.

According to Josephus, nearly 1,100,000 perished during the seven years tribulation: from 66 AD to 73 AD, or 63 AD to 70 AD according to some translations. Among those were not only from the city, but also from out of it, those who fled to Jerusalem when Vespasian wiped out the countryside. Tacitus calculated that approximately 600,000 died in the rebellion. There is a great difference in calculation, nonetheless, the Jewish War wiped out almost every Jewish man and women. Jews became an insignificant minority of the empire. They were to become wanderers of the world for the next 1,850 years.

⌘

4.5. Arrival of Apocalypse

During the seven years of tribulation, Jews saw their social situation as a threshold of apocalypse. Thus, even at the blink of temple's destruction, they held on to their hope that God would intervene at some point. Jews did not necessary look for the end of this world; rather they looked for a strong political ruler – Messiah - endowed with God's providence. Many supported the rebellion because they expected that somebody was going to come out among them to defeat the Romans and save the nation. This prophetic expectation has led more people to be blinded about their current situation. To make a war against such a mighty empire was definitely not a reasonable choice, and if they had been more realistic about the war they would not have made such a foolish choice. The misinterpretation of old covenant prophecies hindered them from perceiving reality.

To the Jews who were confidently assured of prophecies in their favor, defeat was not an option. Ironically, they suffered the greatest tragedy of all time. They lost everything they possessed, including their lives, and not to mention their glorious covenant.

The conflagration of temple was seen as a sign that the apocalypse was about to reach its climax. Those Jews were slain, burned, or brutally beaten. At this very moment, God's house was burning. They must've learned that God no longer dwelt there. They must've thought that God abandoned them.

As mentioned in "Jewish War" chapter, there were false prophets who claimed that God would bring deliverance to those who stood at the top of the temple structure. Many climbed up there, just to be burned up to ashes. It literally seemed as if the world was about to end. But the fulfillment of prophecy was different from what the Jews expected. The fall of Jerusalem was the threshold of apocalypse, which put an

105

end to the old covenant, not the planet earth or the Roman Empire.

The Impact of Apocalypse in Jewish Social Context

This event, which we usually call as "local apocalypse" or "Jewish apocalypse", had its spiritual influence which gave the new covenant men access to God's presence. The new covenant was at last in its completion, to stand forever as an everlasting covenant.

Yet there are other influences of apocalypse, which can be analyzed in different context. This another impact that this apocalypse brought is related with the fleshly nation of Israel, which was the old covenant itself. Israel was a nation, which was administered by the law. She was the old covenant itself. When this covenant was destroyed, it perished along with the Jewish culture, tradition, custom, values and mindsets, not to mention its land and the inhabitants. There were remains of those listed elements, but they were not enough to restore the original Israel prior to 70 AD. Israel as a nation literally vaporized out of history.

Few Jews survived through the tribulation, yet most of their scriptures and holy writings burned with the temple. Without the law, Jewish lifestyle could not continue on.

If everything burned with the temple, then how do our contemporary Jews continue on with their law? Fortunately, Jews were able to retain some of their old heritage. Amid the siege of Jerusalem an aged pupil of Hillel, Johanan ben Zakkai, fearful lest the carnage should destroy all teachers and transmitters of the oral tradition, escaped from the city, and set up an academy in a vineyard at Yabne, or Jamnia, near the Mediterranean coast.[165]

The Transformation of Judaism

Zakkai's effort to preserve Judaism had succeeded to a certain degree, but his achievement was nowhere close to restoring the old covenant that they had prior to 70 AD. Jewish holy writings such as Talmuds that are prevalent today are Zakkai and his colleagues' works.

It was – and is – impossible to restore Judaism as its original covenantal form. First, they did not – and still do not

– have the holy temple. Second, they cannot trace back their tribal lines. Prior to 70 AD, all the priestly works were performed by the tribe of Levi. Now two millennia have passed. How are they supposed to retrace their tribal ancestry? Thus, there was no option left for Zakkai and his friends except to alter the religious doctrine to be suitable for their current condition. Through this alteration, the animal sacrifice was replaced with prayer, and the temple with local synagogues. Without the Levi priests, the Jews have depended upon rabbis for two thousand years.

Judaism took the form that it has kept till our own time: a religion without a central shrine, without a dominant priesthood, without a sacrificial service. The Sadducees disappeared, while the Pharisees and the rabbis became the leaders of a homeless people that had nothing left but its synagogues and its hope.[166]

By undergoing this transformation, Judaism had become a new religion fit for their new situation, and highly efficient for the later coming centuries. It may be somehow cruel, but for Judaism this was a necessary change to be able to survive for next two thousand years. The covenantal aspects perished; instead it became more oriented with daily matters. Their law was developed to be a fine art of living. It is highly detailed, but it also has become convenient in some ways.

The Resolution

Finally, the apocalypse brought major changes to Christianity. It was 70 AD, when the New Testament was consummated. From this point, Christians began to use the early 1st century apostles' writings as doctrines, which later became to be known as the New Testament.

The sack of Jerusalem and its city's entire destruction put an end to a conflict that was prevalent in 1st century church since the establishment of Paul's ministry. Early Christians argued over the center of Christian movement. James, leading the Jewish faction, claimed Jerusalem to be the movement's center. Paul, the head of Gentile ministry, insisted that Rome be the new center of Christian movement. It was the fall - sack of Jerusalem, which decided the future path of Christianity. Christianity was not to remain as a local Jewish sect, but to expand as a global religion.

Christianity in its beginning held a lot of similarities with Judaism. The Romans often confused between the two. Some Christians even insisted on retaining the Jewish aspect. However, after the apocalypse an anti-Jewish atmosphere was created throughout the empire. Thus, from that point on Christians tried to emphasize their differences from the Jews. No longer did they attempt to return to the old way.

Shut out from their Holy City, the Jews were compelled to surrender it first to paganism, then to Christianity. Scattered into every province and beyond, condemned to poverty and humiliation, unbefriended even by philosophers and saints, they retired from public affairs into private study and worship, passionately preserving the words of their scholars, and preparing to write them down at last in the Talmuds of Babylonia and Palestine. Judaism hid in fear and obscurity while its offspring, Christianity, went out to conquer the world.[167]

For Christianity, the non-materialization of Parousia had brought a great crisis to the church. Nonetheless, the earthly temple was replaced with a spiritual one. The hope for Parousia in 70 AD ceased after its spiritual fulfillment. Yet, the spiritual fulfillment granted us life in God's presence. The Holy Place – older tabernacle - was destroyed, the way to the Holy of Holies – new tabernacle – was revealed, which was a way to God's presence. From this spiritual standpoint, the fall of Jerusalem and its resolution was a true birth of Christianity as a fully consummated everlasting covenant.

⌘

5. The Arrival of Christ

5.1. The Olivet Discourse

Within the four gospels, there were only three of the writers to record Jesus' sermon on the Mount of Olives. This sermon is known as 'The Olivet Discourse' because it was a lengthy sermon that Jesus announced there in that location. Although it is not a Biblical term, it is widely known for the description of his sermon that includes all three 'accounts'. The preferred perspective is that from Matthew 24 and 25 because it is the longest and easily divisible, but the information from the speech can be found in Luke 17, Luke 21, and Mark 13. The hermeneutic (or interpretation) of the content has been highly controversial throughout the past ages of the church history. One of the leading reasons is because it contains some prophetic language in which many do not know how to apply them sequentially. Although it seems that my hermeneutic has no difficulty with interpreting the passage, I am in no fashion saying that I have revealed all of the orthodox prophetic meanings in the Olivet Discourse. On the contrary, I am saying that my hermeneutic may make more logical sense than those of traditional perspectives. I have no intention of being boastful about my interpretation, but this is just a simple observation that I have discovered while researching some of the other traditional doctrines.

After the attempt to summarize my interpretation, let us begin to take an actual study with a true, open mind and possibly uncover a portion of its entire meaning. The first passage that comes to mind is the context of the discourse before Jesus begins to deliver his sermon:

Jesus left the temple and was walking away when his disciples came up to him to call his attention to its buildings. "Do you see all these things?" he asked. "I tell you the truth, not one stone here will be left on another; every one will be thrown down." As Jesus was sitting on the Mount of Olives, the disciples came to him privately. "Tell us," they said, "when will this happen, and what

111

will be the sign of your coming and of the end of the age?"[168]

This section is very crucial when setting up the background of which Jesus delivers his speech. The only issue that Jesus describes is while the disciples were looking at the Jerusalem's magnificent temple, and suddenly, Jesus tells them that all of stones of that building will be cast down. Historically, it was documented that Titus' (Roman) army came to Jerusalem during the Jewish revolt, which practically ended AD 70, and we should all be familiar with its events after reading the chapters concerning the Fall of Jerusalem. While this idea was spinning in the disciples' minds, they return to Jesus on the Mount of Olives to discuss this matter in a more serious manner. They proceed to ask him a critical question to this chapter, and the first section of the question asks when this event would occur. This is obvious that when they said 'this' that it was referring to the Fall of Jerusalem because that was Jesus' last statement before they asked this question. While questioning, the apostles used the conjunction 'and' which means 'in addition to' or 'as well as'. In addition to the Fall of Jerusalem, they ask about the signs of his coming, and they ask about the end of that age (KJV declares 'world' instead of 'age', but modern interpreters all agree that the Greek, root word 'aion' should be interpreted as 'age'). Remembering from "Two Audiences of Ministry", which 'age' could Jesus' prophecy be referring to in the scriptural context of the Fall of Jerusalem? Also, what does his coming (Greek, root word 'parousia' meaning presence or arrival) have to do with the end of the Jewish age and the Fall of Jerusalem?

Some theologians have decided that the apostles were asking separate questions in which Jesus gave two, separate responses. The only problem with this idea is that Mark's gospel gives us a different 'version' of the questions asked:

"Tell us, when will these things happen? And what will be the sign that they are all about to be fulfilled?"[169]

While Matthew gives three separate questions, Mark gives us only one question in which the apostles asked. Any division that people try to place within the questions is inconsistently accurate with the parallel passage. Knowing that all the questions asked are unified, what does it mean for the coming of Christ and when was his coming? This simple analysis of these questions would direct to a consummation of all of the events in AD 70 at the destruction of Jerusalem. This statement is only true if the questions were correct in context and if they knew what they were asking. So many have tried to say that the apostles were wrong in their questioning, and Jesus continued on to make his speech on the Mount of Olives answering the questions that they didn't ask. Although this is a slim possibility, how practical would it be for Jesus to give signs and warning (given in Matthew 24:4-35) about the same term 'parousia' asked in Matthew 24:3 to be repeated in Matthew 24:27? Then, he follows the signs with a discussion about the exact day of the end of the age in Matthew 24:36-25:46. As it seems logical, he answers the apostles' questions in the exact order that they asked them, but the only problem comes when people's traditions do not allow all of the final signs and events of the age to be fulfilled.

Jesus directly told his apostles to watch for the signs, but are we the ones to look for them? Absolutely not! As we have stated in "the Context of Scripture", every sermon was designed for a certain audience. After the crucifixion of Christ, four of disciples later decided to write historical accounts that we know today as the 'Gospels' because each different 'version' contains the actions of Christ for superlative doctrinal record. If none of the 'Gospels' survived, then we would have not known the actions of Christ, and we would be considered Christianity without proof. This would not mean that the message of the Gospels would become invalid, but it means that we would have never had the chance to take a look at the 'Historical Jesus'.

Reading further in Matthew 24, Jesus gives the apostles the signs to look for the end of the age, starting at Matthew 24:4-35. Probably the most significant verse of the signs is Matthew 24:14. This verse is where Jesus tells the apostles of what many know of as the Great Commission. As you know, Paul's ministry fulfilled the Great Commission. The sequential time for the end to come is after the Great Commission was fulfilled:

And this gospel of the kingdom will be preached in the whole world as a testimony to all nations, and then the end will come.[170]

If the statement in Colossians 1:23 - that the gospel had been preached to every creature under heaven - is valid, then this end asked about in Matthew 24:3 did come to pass shortly after Paul's announcement of its fulfillment.

Following the Great Commission, Jesus gives specific

directions for the apostles to do when the end comes.

"So when you see standing in the holy place 'the abomination that causes desolation,' spoken of through the prophet Daniel--let the reader understand--then let those who are in Judea flee to the mountains. Let no one on the roof of his house go down to take anything out of the house. Let no one in the field go back to get his cloak.[171]

He tells them if you are in Judea then flee to the mountains, and he is saying this because Judea is where Jerusalem is located. When the Zealot and Roman armies came into this Jewish province, Jesus was telling them to leave the area so that they wouldn't be caught in the conflict. He also tells them not to go back to one's home because if they turned back, then they would be trapped in the city with the same consequences. If Jesus was talking about the destruction of the planet, then it wouldn't make much difference for you to go anywhere because no matter where you ran because the planet's destruction will hit you from anywhere. Either Jesus is incoherent, or Jesus is not talking about the destruction of Earth. Following shortly after these directions, Jesus states this about those days:

For then there will be great distress, unequaled from the beginning of the world until now--and never to be equaled again.[172]

This describes the torment of those who were left trapped inside the temple in Jerusalem. If this great distress about fleeing to mountains from Judea has never been equaled or will never be equaled again, then how can we expect a future destruction of the planet to be horrible about those who are 'Left Behind'? Also, Daniel gives a similar passage about this great distress.

"At that time Michael, the great prince who protects your people, will arise. There will be a time of distress such as has not happened from the beginning of nations until then. But at that time your people--everyone whose name is found written in the book--will be delivered. Multitudes who sleep in the dust of the earth will awake: some to everlasting life, others to shame and everlasting contempt.[173]

Daniel describes a distress that has never occurred since the beginning of the nations, but Matthew's account said that it would never be equaled again. Either Daniel and Jesus are talking about the same event or Daniel's description occurred before Matthew's passage. When we get to Revelation, John is going to describe a similar Judgment and Resurrection that occurs, and John also begins his Revelation saying that all of these things must shortly pass. Without a doubt, Daniel and Matthew wrote about the same the event, which means that John's Revelation was fulfilled at the end of the age.

As the Olivet Discourse progresses, Jesus uses strong apocalyptic imagery to stress his arrival. Notice, the term Parousia is a Greek word that was originally used when a country's king would arrive at a certain location. In the first century, Jesus is prophesying about his arrival as a king in his new kingdom. Notice the nature of his kingdom:

Once, having been asked by the Pharisees when the kingdom of God would come, Jesus replied, "The kingdom of God does not come with your careful observation, nor will people say, `Here it is,' or `There it is,' because the kingdom of God is within you."[174]

Because Christ is coming in his kingdom[175], wouldn't it make sense for the king to come in the same nature of his kingdom? Such imagery is used that it would be visible, but we must differentiate between the physical and spiritual because Christ's appearance must remain consistent. The only way to satisfy all verses concerning Christ's Parousia is to allegorize the images used in Matthew 24. Notice, Christ was not the first prophet to use such imagery. Such as Matthew 24:31 when Jesus is talking about a loud trumpet call, the same imagery is used in Zechariah:

I will bend Judah as I bend my bow and fill it with Ephraim. I will rouse your sons, O Zion, against your sons, O Greece, and make you like a warrior's sword. Then the LORD will appear over them; his arrow will flash like lightning. The Sovereign LORD will sound the trumpet; he will march in the storms of the south.[176]

This does not mean the Lord did these things in a physical nature. This is an apocalyptic description of how the Lord delivered them. This type of apocalyptic and metaphorical language is filled in the Old Testament with many prophets endorsing it so that they would be prepared for the Great Prophet.

Jesus places a time limit on this apocalyptic arrival because he clearly states further in his discourse:

I tell you the truth, this generation will certainly not pass

115

away until all these things have happened.[177]

If you are reading this passage out of a NIV Bible, then the word generation will be footnoted as "or race". This is simply a commentator's remark about the forcing it to interpret as "race". However, this interpretation is not correct because the Greek word used for generation is "genea", and the KJV consistently interprets genea as generation because race has a different Greek word, which is "genos". Although these are similar in spelling, they are not the same term. In the case of Matthew 24:34, genea is used to show that Jesus' generation (Jewish generation spanned for about 40 years) would not pass before all of these things took place. Since Jesus' generation passed at approximately AD 70, then we can conclude that all of those things took place if Jesus is an authentic prophet. Otherwise, Jesus lied and those things did not come in the time for the close of that generation whom he was speaking to. Since there is not much room for other options for meaning of generation, it is certain that Christ's Parousia came in that generation.

Most scholars will agree that Matthew 24:34 was talking about Jesus' generation, but they like to create a division starting with verse 36 to claim that Jesus changes subjects to the end of the planet Earth. The main problem is Matthew 24:21, but there are still other problems.

If there is a division in Matthew 24, then this division must be clearly illustrated in other gospels as well. However, a comparison between Matthew 24 and Luke 17 makes the division in the Olivet Discourse highly implausible, as illustrated in the chart below.

Matthew 24	Luke 17
17 him on housetop	23 look here or look there
23 Look here or there	24 For as the lightning flashes
27 For as the lightning comes	25 this generation
28 carcass eagles	**26 As it was in the days of Noah**
34 this generation	**27 they ate drank married**
37 But as the days of Noah	**30 Son of man revealed**
38 eating, drinking, marrying	31 He who is on the housetop
39 coming of the Son of Man	**35 two women grinding**
40 two men in field	**36 two men in field**
41 two women grinding	37 body eagles

As may be seen, the consequences of dividing Matthew 24 into TWO divisions result in dividing the parallel teaching of Luke 17 into FIVE divisions with a span of 14 verses. How could any of the disciples follow the conversation of Jesus if this is what he did? Are we really to believe this is what Jesus is doing in Luke 17, or is the solution to say that the writer is oblivious to what he is doing as he writes the account as he recalls? To the fundamental Bible scholar, neither choice is acceptable.178

Yet they rely on the fact that Jesus uses the term 'but' to indicate a change in subject, but it really hard to be consistent with that idea when reading the whole gospel(s). Whether or not that is a valid argument, we must think logically of what Jesus was referring to when he just the term 'but'. The passage is as follows:

No one knows about that day or hour, not even the angels in heaven, nor the Son, but only the Father.179

The NIV does not say but as for the day or hour, but almost all other translations do. Jesus uses the word but not to change to a completely different subject, but instead, to finish answering their original questions. Jesus gave signs for his Parousia in Matthew 24:4-35, and he gives details to the specifics of the day in Matthew 24:36-51. He tells the disciples that no one knows the exact day or hour, but the Father in heaven. Then he tells demonstrates how unexpected it will be through his allegory of Noah180. This expecting day would come about the evil and foolish that paid no attention to the signs of the age. Noah did not know the exact day, but the flood did not catch him by surprise either. The same applied to the Christian Jews because the Christian Jews only had signs for the Parousia, but they were never told the exact day. In Noah's day, God waited until everything was complete before he sent the storm. In Jewish age, God waited until the ministry was complete before he sent his destructive army. Peter knew of this and he continues to urge the Christian Jews to remain steadfast in their faith:

The Lord is not slow in keeping his promise, as some understand slowness. He is patient with you, not wanting anyone to perish, but everyone to come to repentance.181

The Lord's patience was with everyone of that age because he did not want any of them to fall. Further into the allegory, Jesus says:

Two men will be in the field; one will be taken and the other left. Two women will be grinding with a hand mill; one will be taken and the other left.182

Just like the days of Noah, the wicked would be slaughtered at the Fall of Jerusalem, and the righteous people who were devoted to their faith would be left to inhabit the Earth. Remember what Jesus said earlier in the discourse:

...but he who stands firm to the end will be saved.[183]

This verse may have a two-fold meaning. The first is that those left would receive their salvation. The second is that they would remain, and they would not be killed in the sack of Jerusalem.

Some people believe strongly that the people who are taken would be 'raptured' up into the physical air. The first problem is that I have already mentioned: it doesn't follow the pattern of the Noah allegory. The second is the disciples ask a critical question about this one being taken and one being left in Luke's 'version':

I tell you, on that night two people will be in one bed; one will be taken and the other left. Two women will be grinding grain together; one will be taken and the other left." "Where, Lord?" they asked. He replied, "Where there is a dead body, there the vultures will gather."[184]

You must decide which person the disciples are asking about when they said, "Where, Lord?" If I told you that I was going to take away one of your pets, the question that would probably to come to mind is: "Where are you taking one of my pets?" I would highly doubt you would be thinking: "Where are you leaving one of my pets?" because you already know that they will remain at your residence. The same applies to this situation because the disciples are curious of where the people would go that are being taken away. Jesus' reply could not fit the 'rapture' scenario because a 'rapture' of the church suggests that they would be taken to a good place (i.e. the heavens, the clouds, etc.) This is the exact opposite of traditional 'rapture' thinking, and I know it is hard to think on terms that are not familiar with your beliefs. However, as long as we are seeking the truth, tradition has no importance.

The Olivet Discourse is one the most highly debated among theological seminaries, but it is the center of Christian eschatology (study of the last things or end times). There have been many reforms in last century because of Matthew 24:34.

If one is to believe that the Olivet Discourse is fulfilled, then many conflicts of previous theologians are resolved. God did not set up his Old Testament prophets to speak in a language to be thrown out later in the New Testament. God used his prophetic language so that only those who are wise would determine its meaning. Peter says it best:

Above all, you must understand that no prophecy of Scripture came about by the prophet's own interpretation. For prophecy never had its origin in the will of man, but men spoke from God as they were carried along by the Holy Spirit.[185]

These prophetic words were written and spoken by men, but the interpretations and meanings are of God's spiritual nature. It would be highly foolish for one to limit prophecy spoken by God to a carnal aspect.

⌘

5.2. On Revelation of Jesus Christ

Not a single Christian would deny that the Revelation of Jesus Christ has been the most controversial book of the entire Bible since the 1st century; its rich symbolism and allegories make it nearly incomprehensible without understanding the framework of the Bible. Many people often ask, "Is there a true interpretation of Revelation?" Yet, it is also the most exciting book in the Bible, because they believe that their future is hidden beneath the pages of Revelation. Modern day theologians attempt every possible means to interpret the meaning so that they could predict when and how Jesus would bring an end to this world. The attitude toward Revelation remains uncertain, wrapped with unknown fear that may come at any moment.

The codes in Revelation are effective – so effective that few people today agree on exactly what they mean. Some people think many of the predictions in Revelation have not yet been fulfilled; perhaps John was writing about events that will come to pass in our own generation, they say. A best-selling book, Hal Lindsey's *The Late Great Planet Earth*, interprets Revelation that way.[186]

Many commentaries dealing with the book of Revelation begin with the first chapter and proceed along; they strive to interpret every single verse in order. Very few commentaries prepare their readers for comprehending the Revelation; that is, to lay out the significance of Revelation in the entire Bible. Also, it is crucial to understand the time setting of Revelation. Finally, a commentator on Revelation must emphasize the connection between Revelation and other New Testament writings. Without proper foundation, a hopeless attempt to interpret Revelation will surely end up with disastrous results. Therefore, it is necessary to build an outline before starting to interpret intricate events.

The Significance of Revelation

There are three elements that should never be neglected in understanding the prophecy in Revelation. First, the transition from the old to new covenant is completed through the fulfillment of Revelation. The way into the new covenantal sanctuary, which is spiritual, had not yet been disclosed as long as the first tabernacle, the old covenant was still standing.[187] The new covenant comes to its fullness after the destruction of older tabernacle. Through the transition, the Revelation should fulfill the purpose of Bible: dealing with the issue of sin and death. How is this transition going to be linked with the Revelation?

As a result of transgression under the law, the judgment plays a significant role in Revelation. It comes as the penalties for disobedience. The identity of Babylon will reveal the judgment's type and its importance when viewed from the entire context. This judgment brings the end to transgression.

Finally, a student must realize that Christ's Second Coming completes the atonement process, which started back at the cross in AD 33. Jesus entered the Holy of Holies of new covenant – or heaven - through his ascension. The writer of Hebrews states: "For Christ did not enter a man-made sanctuary that was only a copy of the true one; he entered heaven itself, now to appear for us in God's presence.[188]" The atonement is not complete as long as the high priest who entered the Holy of Holies remains in there.

Salvation is obtained only through Christ's Second Coming; "so Christ was sacrificed once to take away the sins of many people; and he will appear a second time, not to bear sin, but to bring salvation to those who are waiting for him.[189]" Without the atonement under the new covenant, we do not have salvation; certainly we are not living in God's presence. Only through the atonement can we be redeemed. The redemption comes when the Son of Man comes in a cloud: "At that time they will see the Son of Man coming in a cloud with power and great glory. When these things begin to take place, stand up and lift up your heads, because your redemption is drawing near.[190]" How does Revelation bring the completion of atonement?

Above were three crucial elements in interpreting the Revelation. Briefly speaking, the fulfillment of Revelation must bring the end to sin and death; it must bring the new covenant to its fullness, and God's living presence through salvation. Now it is time to do some background research on Revelation: its time setting.

The Time Setting of Revelation

Concerning the time when the Revelation was written, there are two datings in general. First possibility is the Revelation being written in 68 AD or before the fall of Jerusalem. Another dating rounds off to about 96 AD. First dating is favored by those who see the judgment as that of old covenant Israel, while the ones who favor latter dating believe that the Revelation talks of the judgment on Rome. There is no overwhelming archaeological evidence to prove one dating over another, or at least among my sources. Yet, it is interesting to note that the early churches believed in 68 AD dating. Besides, 96 AD dating would be a very effective tool for some contemporary theologians who attempt to draw away people's attention from 68 AD. They can simply dismiss the whole argument saying: "This book was written 30 years after the fall of Jerusalem!" The most important thing is to understand the significance of Revelation through the book itself and to figure out which dating fits with Revelation's content.

To whom did John send his letters? He sent his letters to the churches in the Eastern Mediterranean. Jesus told him:

*Write, therefore, what you have seen, **what is now and what will take place later**. The mystery of the seven stars that you saw in my right hand and of the seven golden lampstands is this: The seven stars are the angels of the seven churches, and the seven lampstands are the seven churches.*[191]

From chapter 2 to the end of chapter 3, John – who was doing what Jesus told him to do - addresses to seven different recipients and encourages them to endure and wait. John expresses the imminence of Christ's coming in many parts of the letters. In his letter to the church in Pergamum, he says:

Nevertheless, I have a few things against you: You have people there who hold to the teaching of Balaam, who taught Balak to entice the Israelites to sin by eating food sacrificed to idols and by committing sexual immorality. Likewise you also have those who hold to the teaching of the Nicolaitans. Repent therefore! Otherwise, I will soon come to you and will fight against them with the sword of my mouth.[192]

To the church in Philadelphia, he wrote:

Since you have kept my command to endure patiently, I will also keep you from the hour of trial that is going to come upon the whole world to test those who live on the earth. I am coming soon. Hold on to what you have, so that no one will take your crown. Him who overcomes I will make a pillar in the temple of my God. Never again will he leave it. I will write on him the name of my God and the name of the city of my God, the New Jerusalem, which is coming down out of heaven from my God; and I will also write on him my new name. He who has an ear, let him hear what the Spirit says to the churches.[193]

These letters strongly suggest that John directly addressed Revelation to the seven churches, which were going through Rome and Israel's persecution before the fall of Jerusalem. Reading the Bible is similar to reading letters that were sent to 1st century Christians about 2,000 years ago. The collection of these letters is called the "Bible" and we use this book to learn how Christ and his apostles taught the 1st century Christians about the eternal life that they could receive through faith.

Especially in Revelation's case, Jesus told John to send to the seven churches of Asia about the life that they were about to acquire. Yet, some attempt to claim that these letters in Revelation were written specifically for the Christians of 20th century or later centuries. If that is the case, then what is the purpose of writing such passages illustrated above? The seven churches of Asia do not exist anymore! Should we insist that these letters were addressed directly to us, or should we admit that they were addressed to the seven churches of the first century as it is written in the Bible?

There are some theologians who interpret the seven churches of Asia as the seven churches of different centuries. Yet they cannot prove using Scripture that applying seven churches to the churches of different centuries is biblical; they simply distort the meaning to fit Revelation to their futuristic perspective. Without doing so, their whole perspective would collapse.

For such reasons mentioned above, it is both biblical and logical to admit that the time setting is the 1st century, and that John was writing these letters to the seven churches of Asia. By the year 96 AD, there were far more than seven churches throughout the Eastern Mediterranean. This fact indicates that 96 AD dating is very unlikely.

Another biblical source that gives reference to the time setting of Revelation is found in its 10th chapter. John was instructed to eat the little scroll:

So I went to the angel and asked him to give me the little scroll. He said to me, "Take it and eat it. It will turn your stomach sour, but in your mouth it will be as sweet as honey." I took the little scroll from the angel's hand and ate it. It tasted as sweet as honey in my mouth, but when I had eaten it, my stomach turned sour. Then I was told, "You must prophesy again about many peoples, nations, languages and kings."[194]

The good news of the gospel is as sweet in his mouth but its devastating result is bitter in his stomach. The realization of the terrible pronouncements upon his countrymen and the great tribulation, as well as the suffering and even martyrdom of many of the Christians before victory is achieved, was bitter to his stomach.[195]

John was told that he would have to prophesy again concerning many peoples, nations, languages and kings. This indicates that John would survive his banishment to the island of Patmos and that he would still be young enough to carry out his directive. This makes the late dating of the book at AD 96, unlikely in that history relates that John was an invalid by that time and that he even had to be carried to the church. The directive much better fits the earlier dating of about AD 68.[196]

By the fall of Jerusalem in AD 70, the gospel had been preached to all the world as Paul mentions in Colossians 1:23, the hour of Judgment had come. John wrote:

Then I saw another angel flying in midair, and he had the eternal gospel to proclaim to those who live on the earth – to every nation, tribe, language and people. He said in a loud voice, "Fear God and give him glory, because the hour of his judgment has come. Worship him who made the heavens, the earth, the sea and the springs of water."[197]

Just as Jesus said the gospel would be preached to all the world as a sign of the impending end of the age, Paul affirmed that the gospel had been preached into all the world and the end was near. Further, he claimed that his personal stewardship of preaching to all the Gentiles was about to be completed.[198]

John's vision of sending forth the Word – the Great Commission had been fulfilled; it was about time that the judgment was to take place.

Time Setting: the prophecy that Daniel was told to seal up

Back in the Old Testament age, Daniel witnessed the identical apocalypse as John did in Revelation. But this prophecy was not for Daniel's time; Gabriel tells Daniel that the vision is for the time of the end.[199] Later he tells Daniel to seal up the vision:

> *The vision of the evenings and mornings that has been given you is true, but seal up the vision, for it concerns the distant future.[200]*

This vision that Daniel had to seal up is finally revealed through Jesus Christ as he opens the seals of the scroll:

> *But no one in heaven or on earth or under the earth could open the scroll or even look inside it. I wept and wept because no one was found who was worthy to open the scroll or look inside. Then one of the elders said to me, "Do not weep! See, the Lion of the tribe of Judah, the Root of David, has triumphed. He is able to open the scroll and its seven seals."[201]*

Again in the book of Daniel, another time reference is given concerning the end time prophecy:

> *I heard, but I did not understand. So I asked, "My lord, what will the outcome of all this be?" He replied, "Go your way, Daniel, because the words are closed up and sealed until the time of the end."[202]*

126

The prophecy was given to Daniel in 6th century BC. Daniel was told to seal up his prophecy. However, John is told not to. The Revelation was written in the 1st century.

Then he told me, "Do not seal up the words of the prophecy of this book, because the time is near."[203]

After 500 years from Daniel's time, John is told not to seal the prophecy, because the time is NEAR. Since then, nearly 2,000 years have passed. What does this time reference suggest? Daniel was told to seal up the prophecy because of 500 years, why was John told not to seal up the prophecy if the end was to come 2,000 years later? Without understanding the time setting of Revelation, its content is adaptable to the circumstances of every age; as a matter of fact, its interpretations have been applied to the world of every century after the 1st century.

The Uniformity of Doctrine

It should be noted that Revelation creates a compelling parallel with other books in the Bible concerning the apocalypse. The Olivet Discourse[204], 1 Thessalonians 4, 2 Thessalonians 2 all relate to Revelation. All these books are connected with Christ's Second Coming as he brings salvation to those who are waiting for him.[205]

Revelation is also related with the Old Testament prophecies such as Isaiah, Jeremiah and Hosea. These books in the Bible, together with John's Revelation, resembles this marvelous story of eschatology; with the fulfillment of eschatology the transition from the old to new covenant is completed. Due to the transgression of old covenant men, Israel goes through God's judgment; eventually Jesus brings the completion of atonement through his Second Coming. It is astonishing to witness the uniformity of biblical eschatology throughout the Bible. Revelation brings the completion and perfection; its result is the new covenant life that we enjoy today.

⌘

5.3. Covenants in Revelation

By AD 68, the end of old covenant age was drawing near to its climax. Such was the reason for the imminence of end that is expressed throughout Revelation. Through the fall of Jerusalem and the destruction of the Jewish temple in AD 70, the old covenant finally ended. Without the temple, there could be no daily sacrifice, high priesthood and God's presence. The old covenant perished, never to be re-established again.

From Christ's crucifixion in AD 33 to the destruction of the Jewish temple in AD 70, there was a transition from the old to new covenant. In this time period, the two covenants co-existed just as Ishmael and Isaac lived under the same household.[206] In order for the new covenant to reach its fullness, the old had to be cast out.

Revelation reveals to us the nature of these two covenants and how the old one is cast out. With the expulsion of the old covenant, sin and death are defeated. After the end of the old covenant, new covenant age brings life that the old covenant men longed for fifteen centuries under the old age. This transition must resolve the basic problem that began in Genesis, the issue of sin and death.

Two Witnesses and the Flying Scroll: the old covenant?

As mentioned in the 11th chapter of Revelation, God gives power to his two witnesses. They prophesied for 1,260 days. These men had power to shut up the sky so that it would not rain during the time they were prophesying; and they had power to turn the waters into blood and to strike the earth with every kind of plague as often as they wanted.

The identity of the two witnesses has been variously suggested as the Law and the Prophets, Paul and Peter, Moses and Elijah, the Prophets and the Apostles, Zerubbabel and Joshua, as well as others. John doesn't relate the identity of these two witnesses. Was the vision showing the witnesses in the old or new covenant setting? It seems most likely, since the vision is focused on national Israel, that the two witnesses were the Law and the Prophets as depicted by Moses and Elijah. Moses had been the law giver while Elijah had been the prophet. Elijah had begun the line of prophets who called on Israel to repent. John mentions several of the powers these men had been given by God. Moses had turned waters into blood and Elijah had withheld the rain for 3 ½ years. The work of these two men had continued through the Law for nearly 1,500 years.[207]

The great city that is figuratively called Sodom and Egypt, where also their Lord was crucified, can be none other than Jerusalem. Jerusalem had been referred to as Sodom (Isa. 1:10, Jer. 23:14, Ezek. 16:46-52). It was certainly where their Lord was crucified (Heb. 13:12).[208]

*Now when they have finished their testimony, the beast that comes up from the Abyss will attack them, and overpower and kill them. Their bodies will lie in the street of the great city, which is figuratively called Sodom and Egypt, where also their Lord was crucified. For three and a half days men from every people, tribe, language and nation will gaze on their bodies and refuse them burial. The inhabitants of the earth will gloat over them and will celebrate by sending each other gifts, because **these two prophets had tormented those who live on the earth**.[209]*

Note the bold text; these two prophets were torments to the ones who lived on the earth. The old covenant was a ministry of death[210], and it was a curse to the ones who lived under it[211]. Nobody could observe the law perfectly – except Jesus, and it was surely a torment to those who lived under it. This is the very reason why everybody celebrates when the two witnesses died. With the destruction of the old covenant, people are finally freed from the bondage.

Just as these two witnesses represent the characteristic of old covenant, so does the flying scroll mentioned by the prophet Zechariah. Zechariah said:

*I looked again – and there before me was a flying scroll! He asked me, "What do you see?" I answered, "I see a flying scroll, thirty feet long and fifteen feet wide." And he said to me, "**This is the curse that is going out over the whole land; for according*** *to what it says on one side, every thief will be banished, and according to what it says on the other, everyone who swears falsely will be banished. The LORD Almighty declares, 'I will send it out, and it will enter the house of the thief and the house of him who swears falsely by my name. It will remain in his house and destroy it, both its timbers and its stones.'"[212]*

This scroll symbolizes the old covenant, which can be also referred to as a curse. This curse and torment can only end when the old covenant ends. Using two witnesses as a symbol, John prophesies that the old covenant is going to end, with its curse and torment.

The Way into the Sanctuary revealed

With the old covenant's demise, the way into the sanctuary is revealed. It was not open during the time when the old covenant - the older tabernacle - existed. Entering the sanctuary is the major purpose of the new covenant, to be in God's presence. Jesus told his disciples once about his Father's house, and he promised them that he would take them to Himself; thereby bringing God's living presence to mortal men.

In my Father's house are many rooms; if it were not so, I would have told you. I am going there to prepare a place for you. And if I go and prepare a place for you, I will come back and take you to be with me that you also may be where I am.[213]

Under the old covenant, nobody could enter the Holy of Holies – sanctuary – except a high priest and only once a year on the Day of Atonement. It was believed that God dwelt in the Holy of Holies; an old covenant man - who did not have redemption through Christ – could not live in God's presence. Just as the old covenant was a shadow of the new[214], the new covenant had a heavenly sanctuary which no one could enter as long as the first tabernacle still stood. The writer of Hebrews describes the present situation of his time:

By this the Holy Spirit indicates that the way into the sanctuary has not yet been disclosed as long as the first tent is still standing. This is a symbol of the present time, during which gifts and sacrifices are offered that cannot perfect the conscience of the wor-

131

shiper, but deal only with food and drink and various baptisms, regulations for the body imposed until the time comes to set things right.[215]

Revelation brings the completion of atonement; thus it should also fulfill the new covenant men having access to the inner sanctuary of the heavenly temple. John mentions that no one could enter the temple until the great tribulation passed.

*After this I looked and in heaven the temple, that is, the tabernacle of the Testimony, was opened. Out of the temple came the seven angels with the seven plagues. They were dressed in clean shining linen and wore golden sashes around their chests. Then one of the four living creatures gave to the seven angels seven golden bowls filled with the wrath of God, who lives forever and ever. And the temple was filled with smoke from the glory of God and from his power, and **no one could enter the temple until the seven plagues of the seven angels were completed.***[216]

First, what are the seven plagues of God's wrath? Can we find any reference from the Old Testament concerning this passage? In Leviticus, God tells Israelites what He would do to them if they disobey God's law.[217]

*But if you will not listen to me and carry out all these commands, and if you reject my decrees and abhor my laws and fail to carry out all my commands and so violate my covenant, then I will do this to you: I will bring upon you sudden terror, wasting diseases and fever that will destroy your sight and drain away your life. You will plant seed in vain, because your enemies will eat it. I will set my face against you so that you will be defeated; those who hate you will rule over you, and you will flee even when no one is pursuing you. If after all this you will not listen to me, **I will punish you for your sins seven times over.** I will break down your stubborn pride and make the sky above you like iron and the ground beneath you like bronze.*[218]

The judgment was due to the transgression. No one could enter the temple until this judgment passed. This fact emphasizes the significance of Revelation as a completion of the atonement. Entering the sanctuary was possible only when the older tabernacle was destroyed. Yet, at this point in Revelation, nobody could enter the sanctuary; the judgment upon the old covenant had not yet come. The transition from the old to new covenant was not complete. It was to be completed only through the fulfillment of Revelation.

Mark of the Beast; the call for steadfastness

The early church was very vulnerable to the persecution of Israel and Rome, especially to that of the Jews. The Romans did not begin persecution until the very end of AD 60s. At that time Christianity was considered a sect of Judaism, and it was permitted throughout the empire until the reign of Nero. The Jews had been the major persecutors; when the Romans joined Jews in persecuting Christians, the early churches underwent a serious crisis. John warned the fellow Christians not to submit to the persecutors.

He was given power to give breath to the image of the first beast, so that it could speak and cause all who refused to worship the image to be killed. He also forced everyone, small and great, rich and poor, free and slave, to receive a mark on his right hand or on his forehead, so that no one could buy or sell unless he had the mark, which is the name of the beast or the number of his name. This calls for wisdom. If anyone has insight, let him calculate the number of the beast, for it is man's number. His number is 666.[219]

What is the identity of this beast? John gives us a clue that his number is 666. What does this number signify? The answer to this number would solve what his passage actually means. Kenneth C. Davis provides a simple solution to this enigma:

In rock music, books, and films, the number 666 has come to represent Satanism in popular culture. Throughout history, the identity and meaning of the mystical Beast numbered 666 has been applied to such notorious figures as Napoleon and Hitler. In fact, the number has a much simpler and more reasonable explanation. While Satan and the Devil are major players in Revelation, the meaning of 666 was clear to the people of the time. In both Greek and Hebrew, letters doubled as numerals. One simple solution to the 666 puzzle is that the number is produced by adding up the

Hebrew equivalent of "Kaiser Neron," or Emperor Nero.[220]

Max R. King, a noted theologian also gives us his insight on this issue, the identity of the beast with the number 666:

Farrar went on to point out there was scarcely any other living person to whom the Apocalyptic description could apply except Nero; therefore his name would most likely be the first which a Jewish Christian reader would have tried. He said, "accordingly, the Jewish Christians would have tried the name as he thought of the name – that is, in Hebrew letters. And the moment he did this, the secret stood revealed. No Jew ever thought of Nero except as "Neron Kesar," and this gives at once – 50 + 200 + 6 + 50 + 100 + 60 + 200 = 666."[221]
Had a Gentile tried the name Neron in Greek letters the number would have been 50 + 5 + 100 + 800 + 50 = 1005, and the name Neron Kaisar would have totaled to 1337. Hence, by putting the solution in Hebrew, there was less chance of a Gentile enemy's discovering the beast's identity.[222]

Why was Nero such a notorious figure? The Roman society was polytheistic; that is, a pagan society. Romans worshipped their emperors as they worshipped their gods. Many Christians were persecuted because they would not submit to worshipping the emperor. Christianity was not a legal religion in the empire. Thus, there was no legal protection.

The only way to avoid persecution was to worship the emperor or to return to the old covenant way. Fortunately, Judaism was a legal religion of the empire. Jews avoided the persecution for not worshipping the emperor by sacrificing to God in the "name" of the emperor. Of course, the suppression began when the Jewish priests refused to sacrifice in the name of the emperor. The annihilation of Judaism came after four years in AD 70, when the Roman army led by Titus destroyed the temple and wiped out all the inhabitants of Jerusalem.

Jewish persecution was not something negligible, for the Jews persecuted every Christian for not worshipping in the literal temple. This brief period between AD 33 and AD 70 was the most difficult time for Christians. If the early Christians failed to survive through this period, Christianity would have ceased to exist.

John calls his fellow Christians to stand firm through the persecution symbolized by the mark of the beast, because all this hardship was about to end. It would be only a few more years until the old covenant would pass away.

Harvest of the Earth

The event of transition that marked an end to the old covenant was to separate the two covenants typified by Ishmael and Isaac. Paul told his followers that the children of Hagar would be cast out.[223] They were living in the time period when the two covenants coexisted together; they longed for the day when the old covenant would finally be cast out. God's inheritance was that of the new covenant men, not the old covenant Jews.

John symbolizes this event as a harvest, when Christ separates two covenant men from each other. Christ first gathers the new covenant men:

Then another angel came out of the temple and called in a loud voice to him who was sitting on the cloud, "Take your sickle and reap, because the time to reap has come, for the harvest of the earth is ripe." So he who was seated on the cloud swung his sickle over the earth, and the earth was harvested.[224]

After separating the new covenant men from the old one, the judgment comes upon the ones who are left behind. This event is highly identical to rapture[225]; calling Jesus the "one sitting on the cloud" hints us that[226], not to mention the verses listed above. What happens to the ones who are left behind? John described this event as well, because it signifies the judgment upon old covenant Israel.

Still another angel, who had charge of the fire, came from the altar and called in a loud voice to him who had the sharp sickle, "Take your sharp sickle and gather the clusters of grapes from the earth's vine, because its grapes are ripe." The angel swung his sickle on the earth, gathered its grapes and threw them into the great winepress of God's wrath. They were trampled in the winepress outside the city, and blood flowed out of the press, rising as high as the horses' bridles for a distance of 1,600 stadia.[227]

Who are to receive God's wrath? The judgment was to come upon the Jews as Jesus prophesied to the Pharisees, and as the apostle Paul told Thessalonians what would happen to the Jews.[228] It is significant to note that the blood flowed for a distance of 1,600 stadia, approximately 180 miles, which happens to be the geographical length of Palestine.

This Harvest is mentioned throughout other New Testament writings as parables. Few among the ones who read these parables before would have realized that the parables actually meant something more than it did in literal sense. Here are two parables that Jesus spoke of:

Jesus told them another parable: "The kingdom of heaven is like a man who sowed good seed in his field. But while everyone was sleeping, his enemy came and sowed weeds among the wheat, and went away. When the wheat sprouted and formed heads, then the weeds also appeared. The owner's servants came to him and said, 'Sir, didn't you sow good seed in your field? Where then did the weeds come from?' 'An enemy did this,' he replied. The servants asked him, 'Do you want us to go and pull them up?' 'No,' he answered, 'because while you are pulling the weeds, you may root up the wheat with them. Let both grow together until the harvest. At that time I will tell the harvesters: First collect the weeds and tie them in bundles to be burned; then gather the wheat and bring it into my barn.'"[229]

While John used a grape harvest as a symbol, Jesus used the wheat harvest to symbolize the event. This "enemy" may be referred to as "sin", which has power over the old covenant but not over the new one. Although the chronological events are reversed, it should be noted that Jesus spoke in a parable, which was used to give the temple priests some idea of the transition of the two covenants. Jesus also spoke of another parable concerning an identical event:

"Listen to another parable: There was a landowner who planted a vineyard. He put a wall around it, dug a winepress in it and built a watchtower. Then he rented the vineyard to some farmers and went away on a journey. When the harvest time approached, he sent his servants to the tenants to collect his fruit. The tenants seized his servants; they beat one, killed another, and stoned a third. Then he sent other servants to them, more than the

first time, and the tenants treated them in the same way. Last of all, he sent his son to them. 'They will respect my son,' he said. But when the tenants saw the son, they said to each other, 'This is the heir. Come, let's kill him and take his inheritance.' So they took him and threw him out of the vineyard and killed him. Therefore, when the owner of the vineyard comes, what will he do to those tenants?"[230]

Jesus stopped at this point, to let the priests answer this question. Imagine that you are sitting among the Jewish priests listening to Jesus. How would you interpret this parable? First, we should note that the tenants beat, killed and stoned the owner's servants. Why does this sound awfully familiar? What happened to God's prophets when He sent them to the old covenant Jews?

Last of all, the owner sent his son to the tenants. Now it seems much more obvious that Jesus was speaking of his own fate. The tenants said, "Come, let's kill him and take his inheritance." Where do we find this word "inheritance"?[231] The tenants are symbolized as the old covenant men who longed for inheritance but never received it. Only through Jesus Christ could they receive it, but they rejected Jesus and crucified him.

Let's return to the parable: *"He will bring those wretches to a wretched end,"* they – the priests - replied, *"and he will rent the vineyard to other tenants, who will give him his share of the crop at harvest time."*[232]

Who are these "other tenants"? Obviously they are the new covenant men who received inheritance through Christ's glory. As for the previous tenants, God brought them to judgment.

Finally, Jesus clarified this parable to the priests: *"Therefore, I tell you that the kingdom of God will be taken away from you and given to a people who will produce its fruit. He who falls on this stone will be broken to pieces, but he on whom it falls will be crushed."*[233] He told the Jews that the kingdom of God would be taken away from them and would be given to the ones who produce its fruit – the new covenant men. The priests' anger toward this statement is well reflected in the next verse: *When the chief priests and the Pharisees heard Jesus' parables, they knew he was talking about them.*[234]

The above parables create a meaningful parallel with the

Harvest mentioned in Revelation 14. It is necessary, when interpreting prophecies, to go back to other books of the Bible and try to find connections among them. One will be amazed to discover how different writers of the Bible speak of the identical events in many different ways.

Harvest of the earth is an event that separates the two covenants from each other. The period, in which two covenants coexist would come to an end through this harvest. Thus two covenant men walk toward their own fates: for the new one awaits Christ's glory, and God's wrath to the other.

Millennial Reign of Christ

This thousand years reign of Jesus Christ has been a controversial topic in the field of biblical prophecy. Futurism is divided into three branches mainly due to the different interpretations concerning the millennial reign of Christ: postmillennialism, premillennialism and amillennialism. What does John say about the millennial reign?

I saw thrones on which were seated those who had been given authority to judge. And I saw the souls of those who had been beheaded because of their testimony for Jesus and because of the word of God. They had not worshipped the beast or his image and had not received his mark on their foreheads or their hands. They came to life and reigned with Christ a thousand years. (The rest of the dead did not come to life until the thousand years were ended.) This is the first resurrection. Blessed and holy are those who have part in the first resurrection. The second death has no power over them, but they will be priests of God and of Christ and will reign with him for a thousand years.[235]

In verse 4, we see that the thousand years reign of Christ (shared by the beheaded saints) is for the purpose of overcoming his enemies and accomplishing the restoration of all things spoken by the prophets. All things were not put under his feet instantaneously (Heb. 2:8; 10:12-13; 1 Cor. 1:24-28). By the power of his reign, the full end of the old age of sin and death was concluded in the AD 70, demise of outward, fleshly Israel (1 Cor. 15:24; 2 Cor. 3:7-11).[236]

This thousand years reign does not necessarily mean that

there should be a literal thousand years reign, but it seems more reasonable to state that thousand years symbolize the completion of the transition of two covenants, which were the forty years between Christ's crucifixion and the fall of Jerusalem. John uses the Greek word "τελεσθη" whenever he mentions about the "end" of thousand years reign.[237] This word doesn't necessary mean "end", but when translated literally, it is suitable to translate this word into "would be completed", or "should be completed".

Resurrection of the Dead

In order for the old covenant men to come to life, they – the dead ones – had to be resurrected. The old covenant was a ministry of death.[238] Thus, a person who lived under the old covenants was DEAD in spiritual sense. There are two resurrections distinguished with the chronological order. First resurrection that John speaks of in Revelation 20:6 is given only to those who did not receive the mark of the beast – the ones who did not submit to Satan and the beasts. The second death has no power over them, and they are priests of God and of Christ. The old covenant men who accepted Christ as their Messiah – Christians - had come to life through this first resurrection, so that they could become a part of the new covenant.

On the contrary, old covenant men who died before hearing the gospel of Christ or the ones who did not accept Christ during their lifetime were to be judged. They could not participate in the millennial reign of Christ.

The idea of a resurrection is not necessarily reconstruction of physical bodies out of holes in the ground. Ezekiel, speaking of Israel being raised from Babylonian captivity, uses the idea of being raised from the grave possibly much as John may have been using the term "resurrection".[239] Ezekiel wrote:

Then he said to me: "Son of man, these bones are the whole house of Israel. They say, 'Our bones are dried up and our hope is gone; we are cut off.' Therefore prophesy and say to them: 'This is what the Sovereign LORD says: O my people, I am going to open your graves and bring you up from them; I will bring you back to the land of Israel. Then you, my people, will know that I am the LORD, when I open your graves and bring you up from them. I will put my Spirit in you and you will live, and I will settle you in your own land. Then you will know that I the LORD have spoken, and I have done it, declares the LORD.'"[240]

John found the Jews being freed from the Babylonian captivity highly identical to the old covenant men being freed from sin, death and Hades. These freed ones eventually would settle in their new land, the kingdom of Christ that we live in today.

Death and Hades

After the resurrection of the dead takes place, death and Hades are mentioned.

The sea gave up the dead that were in it, and death and Hades gave up the dead that were in them, and each person was judged according to what he had done. Then death and Hades were thrown into the lake of fire. The lake of fire is the second death. If anyone's name was not found written on the book of life, he was thrown into the lake of fire.[241]

This event symbolizes the old covenant men being freed from the bondage. Death and Hades giving up their authorities also means that sin has lost power over the old covenant men. Sin leads to death. Paul explains this concept in his letter to Romans.

Don't you know that when you offer yourselves to someone to obey him as slaves, you are slaves to the one whom you obey — whether you are slaves to sin, which leads to death, or to obedience, which leads to righteousness?[242]

Sin exercises its power only when there is law. Sin does not have power when there is no transgression from the law.

For if those who live by law are heirs, faith has no value and the promise is worthless, because law brings wrath. And where there is no law there is no transgression.[243]

Therefore, death and Hades are destroyed when sin loses its power, and sin loses its power when the law is perished. Paul mentioned the connection among death, sin and law in his first letter to Corinthians. He said, "The sting of death is sin, and the power of sin is the law."[244] Paul's concept of "Death Þ Sin Þ Law" makes perfect sense with John's description on death and Hades being destroyed, the event which signifies the end of sin's influence over the old covenant men, because the old covenant is put to an end.

Passing away of the first heaven and earth

The 21st chapter of Revelation deals with the final stage of covenantal transition. John wrote, "Then I saw the first heaven and a new earth, for the first heaven and the first earth had passed away, and there was no longer any sea."[245] Jesus once mentioned concerning the passing away of heaven and earth; he said, "For truly I tell you, until heaven and earth pass away, not one letter, not one stroke of a letter, will pass from the law until all is accomplished."[246]

Some attempt to interpret the above verse as Christ's law not passing away until the heaven and earth pass away, instead of interpreting the law as the old covenant. They accept that the old covenant passed away, yet they deny that the heaven and earth passed away. Thus, they attempt to change the meaning of the law as that of Christ's law rather than as the old covenant. Here's how NIV translates the above verse: "I tell you the truth, until heaven and earth disappear, not the smallest letter, not the least stroke of a pen, will by any means disappear from the Law until everything is accomplished."[247]

The translators capitalized the word "law" so that Christians would differentiate between the old covenant and Christ's law; if this differentiation was done in other passages, there wouldn't be any problem. But we are dealing with prophetic languages here. They should have been more careful.

If the law, "νομον", was indeed the law of Christ, then does that mean that Christ's teaching would cease to exist after the passing away of heaven and earth? Christ's words are eternal, as Christ himself said "Heaven and earth will pass away, but my words will never pass away."[248]

Above explanation supports the interpretation that the heaven and earth would not pass away until the law – the old covenant – passes away. The writer of Hebrews also mentioned this passing away of heaven and earth, he wrote:

At that time his voice shook the earth, but now he has prom-
ised, "Once more I will shake not only the earth but also the heav-
ens." The words "once more" indicate the removing of what can be
shaken – that is, created things – so that what cannot be shaken
may remain.[249]

The two covenants coexisted together prior to AD 70.
John's account on the passing away of heaven and earth ties
into the passing away of the old covenant, the new covenant –
what cannot be shaken – remains after the passing away of the
old heaven and earth.

Passing away of old heaven and earth was a symbolism
of the covenantal transition; it was also a fulfillment of Isaiah's
prophecy. Isaiah wrote:

> The earth is broken up,
> the earth is split asunder,
> the earth is thoroughly shaken.[250]

> I have put my words in your mouth
> and covered you with the shadow of my hand –
> I who set the heavens in place,
> who laid the foundations of the earth,
> and who say to Zion, 'You are my people,'[251]

The heaven and earth of the old covenant passed away
as the new covenant's heaven and earth revealed its appearance.
John saw the new heaven and earth; the new covenant was
finally brought to its fullness as the old covenant passed away,
and the fulfillment of all these things is concluded with God's
presence among men:

And I heard a loud voice from the throne saying, "Now the
dwelling of God is with men, and he will live with them. They
will be his people, and God himself will be with them and be their
God. He will wipe every tear from their eyes. There will be no
more death or mourning or crying or pain, for the old order of
things have passed away."[252]

Christ's temple and city: Heavenly Jerusalem

God dwells in the temple, and we are God's dwelling
place: "In him the whole building is joined together and rises

142

to become a holy temple in the Lord. And in him you too are being built together to become a dwelling in which God lives by his Spirit."[253] The writer of Hebrews also support the concept of spiritual temple and city as opposed to the literal temple and city of old covenant:

But you have come to Mount Zion, to the heavenly Jerusalem, the city of the living God. You have come to thousands upon thousands of angels in joyful assembly.[254]

John did not see any temple in the city[255], rather it is much more acceptable to interpret that kingdom, temple, mountain and city are identical; they all refer to the spiritual new covenant. It is confusing, because John gave such a descriptive narration concerning the New Jerusalem. What is the significance of John's description? He wrote:

It shone with the glory of God, and its brilliance was like that of a very precious jewel, like a jasper, clear as crystal. It had a great, high wall with twelve gates, and with twelve angels at the gates. On the gates were written the names of the twelve tribes of Israel. There were three gates on the east, three on the north, three on the south and three on the west. The wall of the city had twelve foundations, and on them were the names of the twelve apostles of the Lamb.[256]
The wall was made of jasper, and the city of pure gold, as pure as glass. The foundations of the city walls were decorated with every kind of precious stone. The first foundation was jasper, the second sapphire, the third chalcedony, the fourth emerald, the fifth sadonyx, the sixth carnelian, the seventh chrysolite, the eighth beryl, the ninth topaz, the tenth chrysoprase, the eleventh jacinth, and the twelfth amethyst. The twelve gates were twelve pearls, each gate made of a single pearl. The great street of the city was of pure gold, like transparent glass.[257]

Students who studied Josephus and his writings may recognize that this passage is similar to what Josephus wrote concerning the priestly garment.

The like embroidery was upon the ephod; but the quantity of gold therein was greater. Its figure was that of a stomacher for the breast. There were upon it two golden buttons like small

143

shields, which buttoned the ephod to the garment: in these buttons were enclosed two very large and very excellent sardonyxes, having the names of the tribes of that nation engraved upon them: on the other part were hung twelve stones, three in a row one way, and four in the other; a sardius, a topaz, and an emerald: a carbuncle, a jasper, and a sapphire: and agate, an amethyst, and a ligure; and onyx, a beryl, and a chrysolite; upon every one of which was again engraved one of the forementioned names of the tribes.[258]

It is quite amazing to discover that John's description on the city – or the temple – was identical to that of high priest's garment. From this evidence, we conclude that John's concept of city and temple was spiritual. God dwells among men, and every Christian is God's dwelling. We are priests of God and Christ under the new covenant, John called ourselves priests to serve his God and Father[259].

The Blessing of the New Covenant

The final chapter of Revelation concerns with the blessing of new covenant that comes after the transition of two covenants. The completion of this transition should resolve the problem that began in Genesis: the issue of sin and death. In Genesis, Adam and Eve were driven out of the garden. The angel showed John the river of the water of life, and on each side of the river stood the tree of life. This tree was originally in the Garden of Eden, which means that mankind restores the status of living in the garden.

Revelation's fulfillment completed through the transition from the old to new covenant brings us to God's presence; we reign with Jesus in his kingdom; we return to the Garden of Eden. This transition took place nearly 2,000 years ago; it was completed in AD 70 when the old covenant was destroyed – thereby bringing the new covenant to its fullness. Through this transition, we re-established our relationship with God. Now God dwells in us; we are living in His presence.

⌘

5.4. Judgment in Revelation

Joseph Campbell, a well-known mythologist of 20th century has once stated in his book, *The Hero with a Thousand Faces*: "As the created form of the individual must dissolve, so that of the universe also"[260]. With no doubt, his words reflect the eschatological perspective that has prevailed in men's hearts for ages. People throughout every century have anticipated for the end of the world that they lived in. One did not have to be a pessimist to see the world ending. From the materialistic point of view, this world had contained too many flaws that it seemed natural that someday the world would collapse.

The end of this world was seen as a punishment of humanity's iniquities. As the religions became obsessed with the dualistic view of good and evil, good people – victims – longed for the day when the good would be rewarded and the evil be judged. The result of dualism is the end time madness that sweeps over the nations with the help of media.

For centuries, the concept of universal judgment has had literary inspirations on many different cultures. It should be noted that the major contributor of this judgmental concept to the Western civilization was the Christian doctrine.

This chapter deals specifically with the biblical judgmental concept; studying Revelation from the judgmental perspective will bring answers to many symbolic events that seem ambiguous when viewed from the covenantal perspective. Here are two crucial questions for studying the judgmental perspective. What was the purpose of this final judgment, and to whom was God bringing the judgment upon?

The Purpose of Judgment

From common evangelists to the local pastors, it is taken for granted that Christ's crucifixion in AD 33 has brought the redemption. But the redemption comes after the judgment.

Why are your garments red, like those of one treading the winepress? I have trodden the winepress alone; from the nations no one was with me. I trampled them in my anger and trod them down in my wrath; their blood spattered my garments, and I stained all my clothing. For the day of vengeance was in my heart, and the year of my redemption has come.[261]

The redemption follows God's judgment, Jesus himself also spoke concerning the redemption. First, he said that all the events mentioned in his discourse[262] were to take place at the time of punishment – judgment: **"For this is the time of punishment in fulfillment of all that has been written."**[263] All that had been written at that time – the Old Testament prophecies concerning the end of age were to be fulfilled at the time of punishment. After speaking about signs of the end of the age, he said: **"When these things begin to take place, stand up and lift up your heads, because your redemption is drawing near."**[264] Based on this logic, we state that God intended to bring redemption after the judgment. Thus, the purpose of judgment was to bring redemption.

To Whom, and Why?

Then, why was God bringing judgment? This judgment was foretold when God spoke to Moses and Israelites after giving them the fleshly covenant.

But if you will not listen to me and carry out all these commands, and if you reject my decrees and abhor my laws and fail to carry out all my commands and so violate my covenant, then I will do this to you: I will bring upon you sudden terror, wasting diseases and fever that will destroy your sight...[265]

Therefore, the transgression from the law was going to bring a judgment. Yet, there still was hope. God speaks to the Jews how their remnants were to be if they confessed their sins and the sins of their fathers.

But if they will confess their sins and the sins of their fathers – their treachery against me and their hostility toward me, which made me hostile toward them so that I sent them into the land of their enemies – then when their uncircumcised hearts are humbled and they pay for their sin, I will remember my covenant with Jacob and my covenant with Isaac and my covenant with Abraham, and I will remember the land.[266]

The purpose of God's judgment was to bring the redemption, thereby establishing the new covenant, which we live in today. The judgment was to come as the penalties for disobedience. With this judgmental perspective, we will study the events in Revelation and interpret what significance they may hold. But it is necessary to look at other accounts besides Revelation concerning the judgment, thereby building up the judgmental perspective. Afterwards, the study on Revelation will follow.

Israel's sins and God's judgment

First, we'll examine Isaiah's prophecy and move on to the New Testament writings. Along with Jeremiah's prophecy, the book of Isaiah has an utmost importance of exposing Israel's sins and foretelling God's judgment upon them. Following is a passage that proclaims God's wrath upon Israel.

Awake, awake! Rise up, O Jerusalem, you who have drunk from the hand of the LORD the cup of his wrath, you who have drained to its dregs the goblet that makes men stagger. Of all the sons she bore there was none to guide her; of all the sons she reared there was none to take her by the hand. These double calamities have come upon you – who can comfort you? – ruin and destruction, famine and sword – who can console you? Your sons have fainted; they lie at the head of every street, like antelope caught in a net. They are filled with the wrath of the LORD and the rebuke of your God.[267]
Therefore hear this, you afflicted one, made drunk, but not with wine. This is what your Sovereign LORD says, your God, who defends his people: "See, I have taken out of your hand the cup that made you stagger; from that cup, the goblet of my wrath, you will never drink again. I will put it into the hands of your tormentors, who said to you, 'Fall prostrate that we may walk over you.' And you made your back like the ground, like a street to be walked over."[268]

In the above passage, God's wrath is clearly directed toward Jerusalem; Jerusalem is a representation of the old covenant Jews. Ruin, destruction, famine and sword are the eschatological elements. These are the things that would take place at the judgment upon Jerusalem.

After several centuries from the time of Isaiah, Jesus also spoke of the impending judgment upon Jerusalem. This was the time period when the Jews were about to fill up their cup of sins; through Christ's crucifixion, they completed their wickedness. They were slowly approaching toward tasting God's wrath.

As he approached Jerusalem and saw the city, he wept over it and said, "If you, even you, had only known on this day what would bring you peace – but now it is hidden from your eyes. The days will come upon you when your enemies will build an embankment against you and encircle you and hem you in on every side. They will dash you to the ground, you and the children within your walls. They will not leave one stone on another, because you did not recognize the time of God's coming to you. "[269]

Christ prophesied the fall of Jerusalem, which was fulfilled in AD 70 when this prophecy was fulfilled in the exact manner that Christ told them it would. This was the judgment upon Jerusalem, the old covenant. This judgment put an end to the old covenant, thereby bringing the eternal redemption. Now God's presence is among us, not confined to a certain geographical area.

Ezekiel also spoke of the judgment that was coming upon Jerusalem. His prophecy is a lot similar to Isaiah's. Here's an abridged excerpt of Ezekiel 7.

*The word of the LORD came to me: "Son of man, this is what the Sovereign LORD says to the land of Israel: The end! The end has come upon the **four corners of the land**. The end is now upon you and I will unleash my anger against you. **I will judge you according to your conduct and repay you for all your detestable practices.** "[270]*

*"The day is here! It has come! Doom has burst forth, the rod has budded, arrogance has blossomed! Violence has grown into a rod to punish wickedness; **none of the people will be left**, none*

148

of that crowd – no wealth, nothing of value."[271]

"...*Because of their sins, not one of them will preserve his life. Though they blow the trumpet and get everything ready, no one will go into battle, for my wrath is upon the whole crowd."[272]*

"*Outside is the sword, inside are plague and famine; those in the country will die by the sword, and those in the city will be devoured by famine and plague. All who survive and escape will be in the mountains, moaning like doves of the valleys, each because of his sins."[273]*

"*I will turn my face away from them, and they will desecrate my treasured place; robbers will enter it and desecrate it."[274]*

"*When terror comes, they will seek peace, but there will be none. Calamity upon calamity will come, and rumor upon rumor. They will try to get a vision from the prophet; the teaching of the law by the priest will be lost, as will the counsel of the elders. The king will mourn, the prince will be clothed with despair, and the hands of the people of the land will tremble. I will deal with them according to their conduct, and by their own standards I will judge them. Then they will know that I am the LORD."[275]*

We find many judgmental elements in this excerpt, which are also frequently mentioned in Revelation and Olivet Discourse. One crucial point is, "the teaching of the law by the priest will be lost" at the time of judgment. This judgment is identical to the one mentioned in Revelation and Olivet Discourse; in fact, they all speak of the same judgment, which was to come upon Jerusalem. This was the final judgment that we have feared for two millennia.[276]

Seven Seals, Seven Trumpets, Seven Bowls?

Seven seals, seven trumpets, seven bowls and seven woes all represent God's wrath that was to come upon Jerusalem. Is there any significant meaning for John to use the number seven? What was his purpose of repeating sevens?

When viewed from the judgmental perspective, these sevens are also mentioned back in Leviticus when God told the

Israelites what they would receive if they transgressed under the law. They were going to receive a judgment.

*"If after all this you will not listen to me, I will punish you for your sins **seven times over**."*[277]

*"If you remain hostile to me and refuse to listen to me, I will multiply your afflictions **seven times over**, as your sins deserve."*[278]

*"If in spite of these things you do not accept my correction but continue to be hostile toward me, I myself will be hostile toward you and will afflict you for your sins **seven times over**. And I will bring the sword upon you to avenge the breaking of the covenant. When you withdraw into your cities, I will send a plague among you, and you will be given into enemy hands."*[279]

*"If in spite of this you still do not listen to me but continue to be hostile toward me, then in my anger I will be hostile toward you, and I myself will punish you for your sins **seven times over**. You will eat of the flesh of you sons and the flesh of your daughters. I will destroy your high places, cut down your incense altars and pile your dead bodies on the lifeless forms of your idols, and I will abhor you...*"[280]

Look at the underlined sentences. Do they sound familiar with the descriptions of the fall of Jerusalem? This prophecy in Leviticus was fulfilled when the Romans captured the city of Jerusalem and burned down the temple to its bedrock level in AD 70. From this we know that God was speaking about the judgment upon Jerusalem, but how do we know that this judgment was the identical judgment that was to take place at the fulfillment of Revelation?

Now take a look at the bold text. It seems that God keeps repeating "seven times over". God emphasizes the fact that he would punish the sins of Israel seven times; he would do it again if they do not repent. In Revelation, did the people in the great tribulation ever say that they were going to repent?

John explained in detail the same judgment that God told the Jews about in Leviticus. Why did John mention the twelve tribes of Israel being 144,000? If this judgment is some type of a future judgment other than a judgment upon the old covenant Israel, then what is the point of even mentioning Israel and the temple? These events that are included in the seven seals, seven trumpets, seven woes and seven bowls of God's wrath represent different tragedies that Israel faces at the time of judgment: the judgment upon Jerusalem.

These tragic events such as above are mentioned throughout the Old Testament prophecies. For example, Hosea speaks of the judgment upon Israel:

The high places of wickedness will be destroyed – it is the sin of Israel. Thorns and thistles will grow up and cover their altars. **Then they will say to the mountains, "Cover us!" and to the hills, "Fall on us!** *"281*

How does this single event tie into Revelation? Since the judgment upon Israel, which is mentioned in Hosea, must coincide with other New Testament writings, we will look at Luke's account on Jesus' prophecy.

As they led him away, they seized Simon from Cyrene, who was on his way in from the country, and put the cross on him and made him carry it behind Jesus. A large number of people followed him, including women who mourned and wailed for him. Jesus turned and said to them, "Daughters of Jerusalem, do not weep for me; weep for yourselves and for your children. For the time will come when you will say, 'Blessed are the barren women, the wombs that never bore and the breasts that never nursed!' **Then they will say to the mountains, "Fall on us!" and to the hills, "Cover us!"** *For if men do these things when the tree is green, what will happen when it is dry?"282*

This symbolic prophecy is also mentioned in Revelation:

Then the kings of the earth, the princes, the generals, the rich, the mighty, and every slave and every free man hid in caves and among the rocks of the mountains. They called to the mountains and to the rocks, "Fall on us and hide us from the face of him who sits on the throne and from the wrath of the Lamb! For the great day of their wrath has come, and who can stand?"283

Both Hosea and Jesus spoke of the identical judgment: the judgment upon Jerusalem. Does John speak of the iden-

151

tical judgment with Jesus and Hosea, or is he speaking of a totally different event?

Above presentation was a support for the fact that Hosea, Jesus and John all spoke of the identical judgment. This judgment came as the penalties for disobedience of the old covenant Israel, as mentioned in Leviticus 26. God said repeatedly that He was going to punish the sin of Israel seven times. He continued the punishments upon the Jews until He got to the point where He had to annihilate the Jewish temple and let the Romans massacre almost entire Jewish population who did not come into light of the new covenant. Finally, through this judgment God put an end to the Jewish nation-state and the law – the covenant that He made with Moses.

Earth = Land?

Before moving on to the next subject, I'll have to deal with the issue of translation. It seems odd that particularly in Revelation, the word "earth" is frequently mentioned to suggest a global judgment. The Greek word "γης", which many Bible scholars refer to as the planet earth can be translated as "land", rather than the planet earth. Here's how a NIV Bible translates Revelation 14:6.

hen I saw another angel flying in midair, and he had the eternal gospel to proclaim to those who live on the **earth** – to every nation, tribe, language and people.

In this verse, the word for "earth" is "γης". How is this Greek word translated in other New Testament books? Was there supposed to be a distinction, or is it a result of contemporary Bible translators' bias on the eschatology? Note the following verse's NIV translation.

How dreadful it will be in those days for pregnant women and nursing mothers! There will be great distress in the **land**(γης) and wrath against this people.[284]

Our Bible is often mistranslated due to the map that our contemporary theologians hold. They are the ones who distort the meaning of the Bible to make it suitable for their perspective. It is very dangerous, especially in the field of eschatology, to change the meaning of the word as one desires. Greek is a different language than English; it is hopeless to fit in Greek meaning into English context without altering the meaning of the word as illustrated above. It is important that this alteration is totally dependent upon the translators' perspective.

By referring the land as the planet earth, millions of Christians are being persuaded to expect a worldwide futuristic judgment whenever they read the book of Revelation. It is not spiritually healthy for us to be totally dependent upon the theologians; for every Christian, it is necessary to look at the original scripture oneself and strive to figure out the meaning of it. The Revelation of Jesus Christ has had an enormous social influence over the world for two thousand years in a different way than it was intended to be.

The Mystery of Beasts and Dragon

For the students of Bible prophecy, one of the most intriguing subjects would definitely be the identity of beasts in Revelation. Dragon is already identified as Satan, as John said "that ancient serpent called the devil, or Satan, who leads the whole world astray"[285]. The puzzle lies with the identity of two beasts.

These beasts must be interpreted in light of the 1st century perspective. Today's futuristic millennial views have related these beasts with some political heads of European Union. There are two beasts, one the sea beast and another of the land. The first one represents the Roman Empire that controlled the Mediterranean Sea. John wrote:

And I saw a beast coming out of the sea. He had ten horns and seven heads, with ten crowns on his horns, and on each head a blasphemous name. The beast I saw resembled a leopard, but had feet like those of a bear and a mouth like that of a lion. The dragon gave the beast his power and his throne and great authority.[286]

This description matches with the fact that the Roman Empire ruled the entire known world of that time. The crowns symbolize the kingdoms that Rome had ruled. John's narration also accords with Daniel's prophecy.

After that, in my vision at night I looked, and there before

153

*me was a fourth beast – terrifying and frightening and very power-
ful. It had large iron teeth; it crushed and devoured its victims and
trampled underfoot whatever was left. It was different from all the
former beasts, and it had ten horns.*[287]

Almost all commentaries agree that the above prophecy
of Daniel spoke of the Roman Empire, yet they deny that
John's description of the beast was the ancient Rome. From
their perspective – especially among the dispensational premillennialists, it is a REVIVED Roman Empire, which would fit
with John's description of the beast. They do not realize that
the fulfillment of Daniel's prophecy is ALSO a fulfillment of
John's prophecy, the Revelation.

Daniel spoke of the events that took place after the beast
was thrown into the blazing fire. He spoke of the Son of Man
and the kingdom of God.

*He was given authority, glory and sovereign power; all peo-
ples, nations and men of every language worshiped him. His
dominion is an everlasting dominion that **will not pass away**,
and his kingdom is one that will **never be destroyed**.*[288]

The everlasting kingdom of God comes after the beast,
which creates a parallel with the Revelation. In John's prophecy, the new heaven and earth come after the defeat of Satan
and the beasts.

*Then I saw a new heaven and a new earth, for the first
heaven and the first earth had passed away, and there was **no
longer any sea**.*[289]

John gives a hint to solving the mystery of the beast from
the earth. He said: "This calls for wisdom. If anyone has
insight, let him calculate the number of the beast, for it is man's
number. His number is 666"[290]. The number '666' is a code
known to the priests as Gematria, indicating the names of certain (political) figures. More in depth explanation is given in
the previous chapter. The point is that this number adds up to
"Neron Kaiser", who was a Roman emperor of that time.

Nero – along with other Roman emperors - perfectly
fits with the description of demanding the emperor worship.
Anyone who did not submit to the worshiping of emperors

was persecuted. According to Josephus, the priests in the temple offered sacrifices for the Roman emperors to avoid persecutions. The emperor worship ceased only when the Jews rebelled against the Romans in AD 66.

The Judgment upon Babylon

The siege of Masada, which soon followed the cease of imperial sacrifices, was seen as a sign of Jewish retaliation against the empire. As the rebellion started, so did God's judgment upon Babylon.

It is essential to discover the identity of Babylon before learning the judgment. According to my previous statements, the judgment was to come upon the Jews. Then, why did John record that there was going to be a judgment upon Babylon, not Jerusalem? Are Babylon and Jerusalem different cities? Obviously, the answer is yes. However, are these cities differentiable in context of Revelation? This point, whether they are different or identical, serves as a reference of the judgment's location, and its time setting. "Who is this Babylon?" is the title of Don K. Preston's book; answering this question is the main theme in this chapter.

The woman was dressed in purple and scarlet, and was glittering with gold, precious stones and pearls. She held a golden cup in her hand, filled with abominable things and the filth of her adulteries. This title was written on her forehead:

MYSTERY
BABYLON THE GREAT
THE MOTHER OF PROSTITUTES
AND OF THE ABOMINATIONS OF THE EARTH

I saw that the woman was drunk with the blood of the saints, the blood of those who bore testimony to Jesus.[291]

This is not the first time that this woman makes her appearance. Her appearances are recorded throughout the Old Testament. Here's a scene where an angel shows Zechariah the imagery of woman, from which we can learn the significance of this woman.

155

Then the angel who was speaking to me came forward and said to me "Look up and see what this is that is appearing." I asked, "What is it?" He replied, "It is a measuring basket." And he added, "This is the iniquity of the people throughout the land." Then the cover of lead was raised, and there in the basket sat a woman! He said, "This is wickedness," and he pushed the lead cover down over its mouth.[292]

John uses the imagery of woman in a similar fashion as Zechariah's, in order to depict the iniquities of the people who were to be judged. As a first step in discovering the identity of Babylon, let us look at an incident in Thessalonica. Paul was driven out of the city for preaching the gospel considered by the local authority as disrupting the peace of region. Paul's evangelical activities aggravated the Jews and eventually he was driven out of Thessalonica.[293] After some years, look how Paul recalls this incident in his first letter to the Thessalonians:

*And we also thank God continually because, when you received the word of God, which you heard from us, you accepted it not as the word of men, but as it actually is, the word of God, which is at work in you who believe. For you, brothers, became imitators of God's churches in Judea, which are in Christ Jesus: You suffered from your own countrymen the same things those churches suffered from the **Jews, who killed the Lord Jesus** and **the prophets** and also **drove us out.** They displease God and are hostile to all men in their effort to keep us from speaking to the Gentiles so that they may be saved. In this way <u>they always heap up their sins to the limit.</u> The wrath of God has come upon them at last.[294]*

Paul first identifies the Jews as the ones who killed Lord Jesus and the prophets, and also drove Paul and his supporters out. He announces the final judgment coming upon them; he emphasizes the point that the judgment is impending, by stating "The wrath of God has come upon them at last". Note the underlined verse; **the Jews always heaped up their sins to the limit.**

Jesus also condemned the Jews for their iniquities. In Matthew 23:29-37, Jesus speaks of the punishment that was going to come upon Jerusalem. Below are key verses in the passage:

Fill up, then, the measure of the sin of your forefathers![295]

*Therefore I am sending you prophets and wise men and teachers. Some of them you will **kill and crucify; others you will flog in your synagogues and pursue from town to town**. And so upon you will come all the righteous blood that has been shed on earth, from the blood of righteous Abel to the blood of Zechariah son of Berekiah, whom you murdered between the temple and the altar. I tell you the truth, all this will come upon **this generation**.*[296]

Everybody agrees on the point that in Matthew 23 Jesus foretold the judgment that was to come upon Jerusalem. Look at the bold texts of the paragraph above. That sounds highly identical to the Jews in the 1st century, they who crucified Jesus, killed, flogged and pursued Christians from town to town. The judgment that was to come upon these sinners were all to come upon THIS GENERATION, Jesus' generation living in the 1st century. Note the above bold sentence: "Fill up, then, the measure of the sin of your forefathers."

Now we are back to Revelation. Look at the chapter 18, which concerns the Fall of Babylon. How does John record this event?

*Then I heard another voice from heaven say: "Come out of her, my people, so that you will not share in her sins, so that you will not receive any of her plagues; **for her sins are piled up to heaven**, and God has remembered her crimes.*[297]

The bold text noted above seems familiar. What did Jesus and Paul say? They both said that the sins of the Jews were heaped up / filled up.

In her was found the blood of prophets and of the saints, and of all who have been killed on the earth.[298]

In Babylon were found the blood of prophets and of the saints; what did Jesus say in Matthew 23:35? The below chart might be helpful for looking at the whole picture of this logic.

157

I'd like to thank Don K. Preston for providing this excellent chart[229]; I changed few minor details to improve the impact upon the readers.

Jesus	Paul	Revelation
Prediction and command of world mission (Matthew 24:14; 28:18f)	Commissioned to fulfill the World Mission (Colossians 1:23-26)	Vision of the fulfillment of the World Mission (Revelation 14:6-8)
Mission empowered by miraculous gifts (Mark 13:11)	Ministry empowered by miraculous gifts (Romans 15:19)	Mission empowered by miraculous gifts (11:5-6)
Message of the demise of Jerusalem (Matthew 24 / Luke 21)	Message of the demise of Jerusalem (Galatians 4:22f; Hebrews 12:18f)	Message against Babylon (14:8)
Jerusalem's demise for persecuting the faithful (Matthew 23:29f; 24:9f)	Jerusalem's demise for persecuting the seed of promise (Galatians 4:30-32)	Babylon's demise for persecuting the saints (17:1f; 18:20f)
Jerusalem killed the prophets, apostles and Lord (Matthew 23:34; 23:37)	Jerusalem killed the prophets, apostles and Lord (1 Thessalonians 2:14-16)	Babylon killed the prophets, apostles and Lord (16:6f; 18:20-24; 11:8)
Jerusalem filling the measure of her sin by the persecution (Matthew 23:29f)	Jerusalem filling the measure of her sin by the persecution (1 Thessalonians 2:14-16)	Babylon filling the measure of her sin by the persecution (17:4-6)
Judgment of Jerusalem imminent (Matthew 23:36; 24:34)	Judgment of Jerusalem imminent (1 Thessalonians 2:14f)	Judgment of Babylon imminent (14:7-8; 22:10; 12, 20)

158

According to the parallel displayed on this chart, there can be found a uniform argument among the three narrations. Both Jesus and Paul spoke of the judgment upon Jerusalem. Did John speak of a different thing JUST BECAUSE he wrote Revelation? Revelation was the Revelation of Jesus Christ, as it says at the very first verse of the book. Therefore, Jesus, Paul and John all spoke of the judgment upon Jerusalem, which was to come upon their generation in the 1st century. Otherwise, there should not have been a parallel. In significance, Jerusalem was Babylon of the 1st century.

Satan thrown into the Lake of Fire; the Speechless Guest

As the millennial reign brings itself into the completion, Satan is released.[300] After the final defeat, he is thrown into the lake of fire. Satan's demise means that there can be no more death, that Satan does not hold any authority upon anyone. How can this event be seen from the judgmental perspective?

Jesus spoke of a parable of the Wedding Banquet. This parable summarizes the judgment and Satan's defeat in a nutshell. Note how this parable is connected with the judgment in Revelation.

Jesus spoke to them again in parables, saying: The kingdom of heaven is like a king who prepared a wedding banquet for his son. He sent his servants to those who had been invited to the banquet to tell them to come, but they refused to come.[301]

"Then he sent some more servants and said, 'Tell those who have been invited that I have prepared my dinner: My oxen and fattened cattle have been butchered, and everything is ready. Come to the wedding banquet.[302]

"But they paid no attention and went off one to his field, another to his business. The rest seized his servants, mistreated them and killed them. The king was enraged. He sent his army and destroyed those murderers and burned their city.[303]

"Then he said to his servants, 'The wedding banquet is ready, but those I invited did not deserve to come. Go to the street corners and invite to the banquet anyone you find.' So the servants went out into the streets and gathered all the people they could find, both good and bad, and the wedding hall was filled with guests.[304]

"But when the king came in to see the guests, he noticed

a man there who was not wearing wedding clothes. 'Friend,' he asked, 'how did you get in here without wedding clothes?' The man was speechless.[305]

"Then the king told the attendants, 'Tie him hand and foot, and throw him outside, into the darkness, where there will be weeping and gnashing of teeth.' For many are invited, but few are chosen.[306]

From this parable, first we derive the fact that God symbolized as the king - invited the Jews but they rejected Him. Thus the judgment came upon them; their city was burned. Now God tries to spread the invitation message to the Gentiles. This invitation seems identical with the invitation mentioned in Revelation 22. All that they have to do is to go. Everybody is invited, but Satan symbolized as a speechless guest - who did not own a wedding cloth, gets thrown off the wedding hall.

The Great White Throne Judgment

Judgment is basically to judge a group of sinners according to their deeds. This was the case in Revelation's Great White Throne Judgment. The final apocalyptic judgment was to be completed with the judgment upon the dead.

*Then I saw a great white throne and him who was seated on it. Earth and sky fled from his presence, and there was no place for them. And I saw the dead, great and small, standing before the throne, and books were opened. Another book was opened, which is the book of life. The dead were judged according to what they had done as recorded in the books. The sea gave up the dead that were in it, and **death and Hades** gave up the dead that were in them, and each person was judged according to what he had done. Then **death and Hades were thrown into the lake of fire**. The lake of fire is the second death. If anyone's name was not found written in the book of life, he was thrown into the lake of fire.[307]*

Modern Christians fear that this event implies a future warning that anyone could be standing before the throne, receiving a judgment for what he/she had done. This general assumption serves positively as a very definite, tangible reason to keep away from sinning. But it also brings a negative consequence of lowering one's faith to the old covenant level. We should serve God out of our heart, not from the fear of being punished. Nobody could be justified according to their deeds, and God certainly did not make any type of minimum requirement which determines whether a person be saved or condemned. A Christian should live by faith, not work.

Relying on one's deed produces self-righteousness, which was the case among the Jews under the old covenant. The self-righteousness was the very reason why the old covenant had to be annulled. Nobody was perfect, and a person who boasted to be perfect under his own power, was no different from claiming self-divinity. The judgment came to put an end to this imperfect old covenant and to judge those who were under it.

Anyone who were living under the law were to be judged by the law, as Paul said All who sin apart from the law will also perish apart from the law, and all who sin under the law will be judged by the law.[308] One thing to point out in the passage concerning the Great White Throne Judgment is that <u>each person was judged according to what he had done</u>. Christians are saved in the name of Christ, and every Christian individual's sin is cleansed with Christ's blood.

In Christ, everybody is perfect. This logic draws us a conclusion that Christian is not to be judged. Unfortunately, the old covenant Jews could not atone for their sins without the Savior, and they had to be judged according to what they had done. God recognized their sins as opposed to the sins of new covenant men, which God does not remember, as it is written in Hebrews: "For I will forgive their wickedness, and will remember their sins no more."[309]

Another point to draw from the Revelation passage is that death and Hades were thrown into the lake of fire. After the judgment, there is no more death. But from where does death derive its power? Paul made several good points concerning this issue of death. First, we should realize that the old covenant was also referred to as the "ministry of death".[310]

According to Paul's first letter to Corinthians, death is defeated when the perishable becomes imperishable, and the mortal being immortal.

For the perishable must clothe itself with the imperishable, and the mortal with immortality, then the saying that is written will come true: "Death has been swallowed up in victory."

"Where, O death, is your victory? Where, O death, is your sting?"

The sting of death is sin, and the power of sin is the law.[311]

Sin is also defeated when the death is defeated. Sin was the cause of death, and when sin is gone, there can be no more death. The power of sin is the law. The old covenant served as a measurement to determine whether a deed was good or bad, and anyone who did not follow the law was basically sinning. Sin could not hold influence over men if and only if the old covenant was perished. If sin does not influence men, then there is no more death. Thus, death and Hades being thrown into the lake of fire symbolizes the demise of old covenant.

Putting an End to the Old Covenant

The final judgment put an end to the old covenant and established the new covenant to its fullness by bringing Christ's living presence to the kingdom of God.

Without the law, there is no transgression. Paul said, "For if those who live by law are heirs, faith has no value and the promise is worthless, because the law brings wrath. And where there is no law there is no transgression."[312] God destroyed the old covenant through the final judgment.

This judgment also had been prayed by the martyrs, they had pleaded for their blood to be avenged. The Jews had committed two grave errors: they had forsaken God, and they had killed the prophets and the saints. They certainly did not recognize the consequence of their statement at Christ's crucifixion when they said, "Let his blood be on us and on our children![313]" From the year AD 63 to AD 67, which is 3 ½ years of the Great Tribulation, the Jews enjoyed persecuting Christians, however, the next 3 ½ years would become their nightmare. These Jews could not see the spiritual kingdom concept; Christ was not to rule physically in Jerusalem. There was going to be no literal political Messiah. Much of the religious world has yet to learn this message.[314]

End times concept had prevailed in every civilization since the beginning of this world. Apocalyptic zeal with the eschatological illiteracy among men has led us to believe that there is going to be a worldwide future judgment and many things that are practically impossible. Men make those things possible in the name of God. But God has never intended to bring an end to this world which Himself created with His hands. Revelation does not speak about the planet earth being burned up, but it is about the end of old covenant and the bringing of life under new covenant, which is basically the life in Christ's presence.

⌘

5.5. Atonement in Revelation

Studies on the end times have thrived since the beginning of 20th century. Many books concerning apocalypse were published, and they were always among top 10 bestsellers of the nation in every decade. The most exemplary end times work of this century would probably be Hal Lindsey's *the Late Great Planet Earth,* which was published in 1970. One famous end times book series that had been recently out in the market would be the *Left Behind Series,* written by Tim LaHaye and Jerry B. Jenkins.

Among all the end times books that were published, how many books are there that sees the apocalypse as new covenantal atonement? The majority of Christians view the Revelation from the end times perspective. Very few books deal with the atonemental perspective of Revelation, and even fewer books see the entire Revelation as an account of atonement under the new covenant.

The chapter 1 of Revelation gives a significant hint; Christ is depicted as a high priest. Assuming Christ as the high priest of the new covenant, Christ's parousia must be regarded as the coming of high priest to the kingdom, temple, etc. Yet, the high priesthood of Jesus Christ in Revelation is significantly ignored. For example, Jim McGuiggan summarily regarded the chapter 1 of Revelation as "essentially an introduction in which John says hello to his readers and gives them the occasion for the epistle"[315] rather than reminding the significance of Christ's high priesthood. Later he does mention Christ's imagery, as that of the high priest, but it is not a crucial point of his argument.

The contemporary Christians are succumbed to the physical, literal fulfillment of Bible prophecy. After the publication of *Left Behind Series*, many pastors should agree that their church members are increasingly demanding more studies on Revelation. The general public is thirst for more knowledge behind the end times issue, but how many among all the pastors of America can teach their congregations that the book of Revelation is an atonement through which we receive our salvation?

Revelation as the new covenantal atonement is the main argument of this chapter. This perspective must be considered as the most crucial among all three perspectives since it is directly connected with the issue of our salvation. Without the fulfillment of Christ's parousia, there can be no salvation. In simple words, Christians cannot say, "We are saved" until the return of Jesus Christ. As the writer of Hebrew wrote: "so Christ was sacrificed once to take away the sins of many people; and he will appear a second time, not to bear sin, but to bring salvation to those who are waiting for him."[316]

Christ as the High Priest

John saw the Son of Man "dressed in a robe reaching down to his feet and with a golden sash around his chest."[317] Why was Jesus dressed in a priestly garment? He was the high priest in covenantal significance; Jesus was the one who was performing the atonement. The crucifixion must be regarded as the sacrifice – a process in the atonement. Jesus is the last among all the high priests that came under the old covenant.

Christ's priesthood was the point that John made when

he wrote of imageries of the Son of Man as a high priest. The salvation comes only after Jesus serves as a high priest to perform the atonement. This final atonement – that of the new covenant, was what John portrayed in Revelation of Jesus Christ. Although shrouded with symbolism and apocalyptic language, what John constructed as a framework of Revelation was the general overview of the atonement for redemption, thereby obtaining salvation, also known as the water of life.

For this reason, we Christians have a right to say that we are saved through Christ; Jesus was the one who performed the atonement. This simple, yet vital logic is what our contemporary Christianity lacks; it demonstrates how theology can be effectively used to support and lead the Christian faith. Without the proper theology, Christian evangelism has remained in its most primitive form. It is time to recognize Christ's priesthood to lead the Christians to re-focus their attentions on the new covenantal atonement and its completion through the fulfillment of Revelation. In the beginning chapter of Revelation, why did John see Jesus as the high priest? This fact may give some ideas to our readers.

The Heavenly Worship: God's heavenly temple

After sending the letters to the seven churches of Asia, John is called forth into the heavenly realm to witness what must soon take place. This scene would serve to give much needed encouragement to the persecuted saints. The combined persecution of the Romans, under Nero and the nation of Israel had brought Christianity to its knees. This magnificent rendering of the throne scene and the ensuing victory of God's new covenant people would help encourage the Christians to remain faithful even if it cost them their physical lives.[318]

Who are these twenty-four elders[319]? The elders probably represent the Old Testament priesthood as it was divided into twenty-four courses of twenty-four priests in each one.[320] It was required that there be twenty-four priests on duty at any given time. The book of Revelation uses much of the imagery of the old covenant. The items under the old covenant were but a shadow of the reality that was unfolding under the new covenant. Under the new covenant, the priesthood consists of all Christians and is referred to as a "royal priesthood" (1 Peter

2:9).[321]

Concerning the appearance of these elders, John said "They were dressed in white and had crowns of gold on their heads".[322] Is there any Old Testament passage that matches with John's imagery? How did the old covenant priesthood appear to be?

> *Then Moses brought Aaron and his sons forward and washed them with water. He put the tunic on Aaron, tied the sash around him, clothed him with the robe and put the ephod on him. He also tied the ephod to him by its skillfully woven waistband; so it was fastened on him. He placed the breastpiece on him and put the Urim and Thummim in the breastpiece. Then he placed the turban on Aaron's head and set the gold plate, the sacred diadem, on front of it, as the LORD commanded Moses.[323]*

The above description of the high priestly garment sounds very similar to what John said about the garments of twenty-four elders. John derived not only the appearance but also the significance of the elders from the high priests of the old covenant.

So, what was John's crucial point in mentioning the twenty-four elders? Let us realize that they represented the royal or kingly priesthood of Christ[324]. Since the symbolisms of Revelation are primarily from the Old Testament, a search of that typical priesthood should supply the answer desired. In 1 Chronicles 24:1-19, David divided the priesthood into twenty four courses, choosing sixteen chief men of the sons of Eleazar and eight chief men of the sons of Ithamar "for the governors of the sanctuary.[325]" These twenty-four governors or princes represented the entire priesthood of Israel, and therefore the number twenty-four in Revelation is a fitting symbolical representation of the *royal priesthood* redeemed by the blood of the Lamb.[326]

Concerning the atonement, nothing is more significant than the priesthood. And by the time Revelation was given, this priesthood was about to be transformed from a mere pattern to a powerful eternal one that was coming through Jesus Christ's parousia.

Sealing of 144,000; the Great Multitude

168

There are many prophecy teachers who interpret this number as being symbolic, although there are others who believe this should be interpreted literally - not to mention the Jehovah's Witnesses. They know the significance of 144,000 representing the tribesmen of Israel. From the contemporary premillennial perspective, the 144,000 witnesses are often referred to as the "converted Jews".

There shouldn't be any distinction between the Jews and Gentiles once they come into Christ's presence. Believing that there will be mass conversions in the Jewish communities to Christianity is not a bad idea, but it is necessary to point out that this expectation of Jewish converts was a distinct social element, which was only existent back in the 1st century. Visiting Jewish synagogues was a daily activity for the apostles, especially Paul, unlike our 20th century evangelists who are content with their belief that Jews are God's chosen people.

Another point is that there hardly is any pure Jewish ethnicity. After the Jewish apocalypse in 70 AD, Israel as a nation-state was shattered as did many parts of their hereditary custom – although they still claim to retain their culture prior to the fall of Jerusalem. For example, there is not a single Jewish person who can re-trace back their tribal ancestry. Some biologists work to re-trace the blood type of different tribesmen who lived back 2,000 years ago. But unless those people living back in 1st century took blood tests, there cannot be any standard of measurement for such biological testing. A pure tribesman of Levi is a necessity to re-build the old covenantal high priesthood; unless they make some adjustments to their religious doctrine, Jews will never have a high priest. Of course, one particular premillennial expectation of converted Jews from each tribe of Israel with equal number – 12,000 - is an implausible justification to their doctrine.

Then, what happens to the premillennial philosophy of "literal interpretation"? The 1st century social elements such as the tribal identity cannot be reproduced in any other century that comes after the 1st century. It is much more reasonable to admit that the number 144,000 is symbolic; the followers of Christ in Israel, who were still influenced by the old covenant, going through the persecutions were to be assured that they were to be saved from the horror of apocalypse in 70 AD.

A great multitude that follows the sealing of 144,000 must be interpreted as the ones regardless of ethnicity who were being persecuted throughout the 1st century world – the Roman Empire. They all "washed their robes and made them white in the blood of the Lamb"[327]. Also, it should be pointed out that they were wearing robes as if they were priests. Everybody wears a robe, which reflects the concept of universal priesthood. The new covenantal atonement influences everyone who is in Christ, and everyone who is under Christ is also a priest of new covenant. John first mentioned this concept in the beginning of Revelation as he glorified Christ.

To him who loves us and has freed us from our sins by his blood, and has made us to be a kingdom and priests to serve his God and Father – to him be glory and power for ever and ever! Amen.[328]

By describing the eternal atonement that only comes through Christ, Revelation serves as a reminder that we are God's priests, and that we are holy in Christ. Nothing is more helpful for building faith in Christ than to know about the atonement done by him. Revelation was an effective encouragement to the Christians who were under the persecutions; they held on firmly to their expectation of Christ's salvation through his parousia. The worldwide Christian faith we have today is a result of 1st century Christianity's steadiness. Without this Revelation, such accomplishment would not have been possible.

The Seventh Seal

Another element of the atonement is found in Revelation, the seventh seal is actually a part of atonement process. Seventh seal triggers the sounding of trumpets, which was also performed as a part of atonement. But the imagery that comes after it cannot be referred other than as an atonemental ritual.

And I saw the seven angels who stand before God, and to them were given seven trumpets. Another angel, who had a golden censer, came and stood at the altar. He was given much incense to offer, with the prayers of all the saints, on the golden altar before the throne. The smoke of the incense, together with the prayers of the saints, went up before God from the angel's hand. Then the angel took the censer, filled it with fire from the altar, and hurled it on the earth; there came peals of thunder, rumblings, flashes of lightning and an earthquake.[329]

Our 20th century Christians are so focused upon the visual impact of the event that they tend to ignore the significance of this event in the atonement as a whole. How could this have been perceived from the atonemental perspective of Moses?

Aaron shall bring the bull for his own sin offering to make atonement for himself and his household, and he is to slaughter the bull for his own sin offering. He is to take a censer full of burning coals from the altar before the LORD and two handfuls of finely ground fragrant incense and take them behind the curtain. He is to put the incense on the fire before the LORD, and the smoke of the incense will conceal the atonement cover above the Testimony, so that he will not die. He is to take some of the bull's blood and with his finger sprinkle it on the front of the atonement cover; then he shall sprinkle some of it with his finger seven times before the atonement cover.[330]

We find that the Revelation's seventh seal is actually the replay of a phase in the past atonement process described in Leviticus. Just imagine the atonement scene displayed in a grand scale through the fulfillment of Revelation! There is a distinction between the atonements of the past and the final atonement, that although the past atonements were simply "reminders of the sin", the final atonement which comes through Christ is eternal. Our vision being enslaved to physical realm simply hinders us from understanding the significance; what matters is the spiritual significance, not a physical one.

The Seven Trumpets

In light of the atonemental perspective, these trumpets also must be interpreted as a part of the atonement. They also are related with the resurrection of the dead. First, what part of the atonement do the seven trumpets represent?

Then he shall come out to the altar that is before the LORD and make atonement for it. He shall take some of the bull's blood and some of the goat's blood and put it on all the horns of the altar. He shall sprinkle some of the blood on it with his finger seven times to cleanse it and to consecrate it from the uncleanness of the Israelites.[331]

Symbolic imageries such as the seven trumpets are actually simple steps in the atonement. But the final atonement was to be performed in supernatural manner, which we do not have any record – except few historical accounts before the fall of Jerusalem. To find the visually displayed signs such as those including the seven trumpets, read the chapters concerning the fall of Jerusalem. According to the historians of 1st century, there were many unexplainable signs that preceded the fall of Jerusalem, which sound highly identical to the imageries of Revelation.

Another significance of these trumpets is that the seventh trumpet serves as a signal for the resurrection of the dead. There are two New Testament passages that I will cover concerning this topic, which are written by the apostle Paul.

For the Lord himself will come down from heaven, with a loud command, with the voice of the archangel and with the trumpet call of God, and the dead in Christ will rise first.[332]

Another passage comes from Paul's first letter to the church in Corinth: "in a flash, in the twinkling of an eye, at the last trumpet. For the trumpet will sound, the dead will be raised imperishable, and we will be changed."[333] For both passages, Paul mentions the trumpets and the resurrection of the dead follows. Therefore, triggering the resurrection was also another significance of the trumpets.

Every eye shall see him?

Our traditional concept of Christ's parousia, which also has been addicted to the literal, fleshly expectation of the fulfillment, has led us to be merely focused on this supposed physical phenomenon than its spiritual significance. The picture illustrated below would be a suitable representation of what most Christians believe that is going to happen.

Christ physically comes on the clouds of the sky; believers are raptured, those who did not believe in Christ are left behind to suffer God's wrath, etc. That is how we would briefly summarize the traditional concept of parousia; coincidentally, this description is simply a visual portrayal of how people think this event is going to take place. Although every Christian is so intrigued with the manner of the fulfillment of this phenomenon, very few among them attempt to find the significance of it. One main reason that caused this eschatological illiteracy would be the method that these Christians read the Bible. Taking the words at face value may help in using Bible for everyday application purpose, however such method is inappropriate when interpreting the original meaning in historical context.

Similarly, same principle applies with the prophecies in Revelation. Let us examine what John stated concerning Christ's parousia.[334]

Look, he is coming with the clouds, and every eye will see him, even those who pierced him; and all the peoples of the earth will mourn because of him. So shall it be! Amen.[335]

First, let's assume that this phrase demands a literal, fleshly fulfillment. From this point, we will take two different approaches in interpreting this event besides the atonemental perspective. We can either look from a historical perspective, a deconstructive perspective, or both.

When interpreting the writing from a historical – or even a new historical – perspective, it is necessary that a literary work be read with a sense of the time and place of its creation, because every literary work is a product of its time and its world. Understanding the social background and the intellectual currents of that time and that world illuminate literary works for later generations of readers.[336]

Keep being informed that John was a 1st century Jew, who had a lot of knowledge in the old covenant scripture – the Holy Spirit gave him the knowledge. Considering that Revelation is the final book of the Bible, which concludes every book that preceded it, it is natural that its content be somehow related with every eschatological material that was given. Thus, the Revelation took the form of Jewish apocalyptic literature to express its meaning and significance. It has been demonstrated through the countless examples from the Old Testament prophecies that I provided. The point is that this "every eye shall see him" concept was derived somehow from some of Old Testament prophecies. The prophet Isaiah spoke of the same literary style that John used in Revelation.

*A voice of one calling; "In the desert prepare the way for the LORD; make straight in the wickedness a highway for our God. Every valley shall be raised up, every mountain and hill be made low; the rough ground shall become level, the rugged places a plain. And the glory of the LORD will be revealed, and **all mankind together will see it**. For the mouth of the LORD has spoken."*[337]

The first half of this prophecy was fulfilled through John the Baptist. The gospel writer Luke recorded this event – it is also recorded at John 1:23. Luke 3:4 illustrates Isaiah's prophecy being in process to its fulfillment, although it didn't involve any physical phenomenon such as the terrain being altered through some sort of supernatural force. This proves that the Jewish apocalyptic literature did not necessitate a literary fulfillment to a symbolic prophecy.

It would be very difficult especially to the advocates of literal interpretation that a language may mean something different than the way it is written. But it should be noted that a language could be deconstructed to a point where its meaning is not what it says in its literal sense. This is a type of deconstructive perspective that we are taking in this case.

Deconstructionist critics operate on the premise that language is irretrievably self-contradictory and self-destroying. They argue that since language is unstable, it cannot be controlled by writers. As a result, literary works mean more than their authors are aware of – which was definitely the case of John where Holy Spirit was actually working through him, and their meanings are as unstable as the language of which they are constructed. The aim of deconstructive analysis is to demonstrate the instability of language in texts, thereby revealing how a text's conflicting forces inevitably destroy its apparently logical or meaningful structure and how its apparently clear meaning splits into contradictory, incompatible, and ultimately undecidable possibilities.[338]

As the deconstructive perspective illustrates, it is possible that John's words do not actually reflect the apparent meaning of the passage. Instead, if it is taken literally, it could be a conflicting point with other parts of the Bible. How is this possible?

First, note that every eye was going to see Jesus coming on clouds, even those who pierced him. If this coming was to be fulfilled 2,000 years after His ascension, then how are these Romans soldiers – who pierced him – supposed to survive to see the coming of the Lord? Now the literal interpretation demands an implausible justification to fit the prophecy into their map. Even if those Romans soldiers are resurrected at the end of age, sadly the resurrection of the dead occurs AFTER the parousia, as it is illustrated in 1 Thessalonians 4:16. Same situation takes place with Jesus' conversation with the high priest Caiaphas.

> *...Jesus remained silent. The high priest said to him, "I charge you under oath by the living God: Tell us if you are the Christ, the Son of God." "Yes, it is as you say," Jesus replied. "But I say to all of you: In the future you will see the Son of Man sitting at the right hand of the Mighty One and coming on the clouds of heaven.*[339]

Personally, I have a problem with the NIV translation. I suggest you to look up this verse with other translations such as NRSV or Greek-English Interlinear. The point is that Matthew 26:64, along with Revelation 1:7 give a reference to when this would take place.

Another point: the Kingdom of God was supposed to come at the parousia[340]. If this coming must be a visible occurrence, then so does the Kingdom of God. But what did Jesus say concerning the coming of His kingdom? Luke's account tells how Jesus dismissed the Pharisees' physical concept, which is still prevalent among the majority of Christians today.

> *Once, having been asked by the Pharisees when the kingdom of God would come, Jesus applied, "The kingdom of God does not come with your careful observation, nor will people say, 'Here it is,' or 'there it is,' because the kingdom of God is within you."*[341]

Jews rejected Christ, because they were blinded by the physical, fleshly expectation of the king that they could not comprehend Christ's spiritual significance. Unfortunately, even though we are living in Christ's presence, we are not conscious of the fact due to our expectation of the literal fulfillment.

Confirmation of the Atonement

If Christ's second coming must not be regarded as a physical phenomenon, then what significance does this prophecy[342] hold? This event should be interpreted through the atonemental perspective; it should be regarded as a phase of the atonement through which Christ completes the entire atonement process. Without the confirmation of the atonement, there is no redemption. Until the high priest enters the Holy of Holies and comes out to confirm that the multitude's sin has been forgiven, the atonement has no significance. Under the new covenantal atonement, Christ was to return from the Holy of Holies to take us to His – God's Presence. First, let us look at a pattern of the atonement under the old covenant.

No one is to be in the Tent of Meeting from the time Aaron goes in to make atonement in the Most Holy Place until he comes out, having made atonement for himself, his household and the whole community of Israel.[343]

The entire atonement, which takes place in Revelation, is fulfilled through Christ's parousia. His coming confirms that we receive our salvation through Christ. Every eye seeing his coming is a literary description of the confirmation of this atonement, which was completed in AD 70 when the old covenant was put to an end; thereby opening a way to the heavenly sanctuary[344].

Obtaining the Salvation

Salvation comes as the atonement is completed through its confirmation, Christ's parousia. Many Christians believe that they already have salvation; yet they still wait for the future coming of Christ. Is it possible that we are still waiting for the salvation if we expect a future, fleshly return of Jesus Christ?

...so Christ was sacrificed once to take away the sins of many people; and he will appear a second time, not to bear sin, but to bring SALVATION to those who are waiting for him.[345]

Christ's crucifixion served as a sacrifice necessary for enabling the atonement process; this atonement process is finally completed as Christ appears again. Without the confirmation – the parousia, we do not have salvation: we are still waiting for it. There is a huge difference between having the salvation and waiting for the salvation. Although our contemporary Christians often refer to themselves as the "saved ones", they should also acknowledge Christ's parousia in order to declare themselves to be saved.

This salvation that we have in Christ is also a restoration of what Adam and Eve lost in the garden of Eden. The crucial significance of the fall of men is that men lost their relationships with God. Fallen men are disconnected from God; they are living out of God's presence. The whole Bible is an epic struggle of mankind striving to achieve one final goal: being in God's living presence. Living in God's presence is the salvation that we have through Jesus Christ; this presence of God is what our humanity had longed for since the creation of this world, which came when the old covenant was destroyed and the new covenant firmly established – the time of Revelation's fulfillment.

And I heard a loud voice from the throne saying, "Now the dwelling of God is with men, and he will live with them. They will be his people, and God himself will be with them and be their God. He will wipe every tear from their eyes. There will be no more death or mourning or crying or pain, for the old order of things has passed away."[346]

From the eschatological viewpoint, we can first identify God's presence among men, and that there is no more death. Death came through the ministry that was engraved in letters on stone.[347] And when this old order – the old covenant, also known as the ministry of death, is passed away, there is no more death according to what a loud voice from the throne said. In spiritual sense, living out of God's presence was basically death. After Adam and Eve were driven out of the garden, this was the type of death, which our mankind had suffered since the creation of this world until Christ came to set us free. Eventually, the new covenant men receive salvation through Christ's parousia, which had been fulfilled in AD 70 when the covenantal transition, the judgment upon Babylon – Jerusalem – and Christ's atonement were complete.

The theme, which sums the entire Bible from Genesis to

Revelation, is put into simple, concise words. The one seated on the throne said, "It is done. I am the Alpha and the Omega, the Beginning and the End. To him who is thirsty I will give to drink without cost from the spring of the water of life. He who overcomes will inherit all this, and I will be his God and he will be my son."[348] Through the completion of atonement, we receive life from God, and we become God's children. From that point on we have a right to call God our "Father". Although our contemporary churches do not acknowledge the fulfillment of Revelation, yet they hold and practice many aspects that they are supposed to acquire after the fulfillment of all things.

It is time we Christians realize the significance of the fulfillment of Revelation. Without the completion of atonement, first we do not have salvation but still waiting for it. Second, we are not God's children. Third, we do not have life – the life in God's presence. However, the fulfillment, or the completion of atonement is what brings us the benefits that the people under the old covenant could not receive. Here's my last question for you to reconsider: "Do we have salvation, which brings us life in God's presence, or are we still waiting for it?"

⌘

6. Neo-Reformation

6.1. Historical Reformation

Human history is all about the continuation of conflicts between old and new, the change versus traditional stability. These conflicts have existed in every aspect of civilizations throughout the ages. Change begins usually from a relatively enlightened individual or group of individuals, and from these people the new ideas are born. Some of these ideas are true, while others may be false.

Whenever a social change occurs, it should face fierce oppositions from traditionalists. Traditionalists in this sense are individuals who favor stability over the benefits given through the change. In historical sense, they are defined as conservatives, or reactionaries.

Traditionalists contend that the position they hold is supported by the majority of people and this is their strongest motivation to oppose new ideas, because relatively few people believe in new ideas. They do not realize that by closing their minds they may be ignoring the truth or a change that is the necessity of humankind.

Such incidents took place throughout our history and some are still taking place. For example, when Copernicus presented the geocentric conception, his new theory was responded with scorn and skepticism. No revolution occurred overnight. Nevertheless, now we all know that the earth revolves around the sun, not the sun revolving around the earth.

When the French revolution started, many Europeans expected it to die off in few months, however this newborn republic survived despite oppositions from the rest of Europe. After two centuries, the French revolution stands as a cornerstone for world democracy. Democratic ideas are accepted worldwide.

These examples prove that the struggle for truth, or the necessity for change, always triumph over the tradition. If that

181

is the case, then what examples are there in the Christian history? I already mentioned in the prologue about the Protestant Reformation, which was a worldwide conflict between the truth and tradition. Such incidents also took place in the 1st century as the Christians continued to hold fast while the Jews suppressed and persecuted this new "heresy". For instance, Jesus told the Pharisees, "You have a fine way of rejecting the commandment of God in order to keep your tradition!"[349] Why did the Jews reject Jesus Christ? It is because the scribes and priests contended on tradition and insisted that they – the majority – could never be wrong. Does this sound familiar to you? What happened to the Jews who crucified Jesus Christ?

Insisting on the fulfillment of parousia in AD 70 may seem highly radical when viewed from the contemporary tradition, however, it should be noted that the 1st century Christians believed the parousia to take place in their "generation"[350]

Contemporary theologians assert that the kingdom had been postponed, which means that it did not take place despite Jesus and His apostles expected it to come in their generation. By doing this, they oppose Christ and the Holy Spirit who wrote the Bible. Is this the right path that the Christians should be taking? Should we believe the contemporary theologians, or should we believe God?

⌘

6.2. Classical and Contemporary Millennialism

How does the 1st century eschatology differ from the contemporary eschatology? It is quite simple. The 1st century Christians believed the Parousia to take place within the generation of Jesus' contemporaries, the contemporary theologians believe that it will take place within our generation, or at any moment.

Christ Himself believed that His Second Coming was to be fulfilled within His generation, not ours. Knowing Jesus' time statements is crucial in understanding the time of Parousia's fulfillment.

The Delay of Parousia???

Jody, my church's preacher lent me two commentaries on the books of James and Jude. While skimming through the pages, I happened to find an interesting passage to note. James 5:8 states, "You too, be patient and stand firm, because the Lord's coming is near." What did he mean by that? Here's what the commentator wrote:

> Christians, like the farmer, must wait patiently for the blessing of the Lord (cf. Psalm 37). They are to stand firm (literally "to strengthen their hearts," cf. 1 Thessalonians 3:13; 2 Thessalonians 2:17) for the ultimate blessing of the Lord's coming is near. Jesus and his disciples often said the kingdom was near (Matthew 4:17; 10:17; Mark 1:15; Luke 10:9; 11; Romans 13:12; Hebrews 10:25, 37; 1 Peter 4:7).
>
> What did they mean? Many of the early Christians expected Jesus to return in their lifetime. Now it has been almost 2000 years since he promised to return. Can one still say Jesus is coming soon, and the end is near? Yes, for we do not know when he will come.[351]

In other words, this commentator is saying that the 1st century Christians' expectation faded in vain. However, many critics and skeptics of Christianity put more faith on 1st century Christians than relying on the contemporary theologians. Among these critics, there was a man named Albert Schweitzer. He is often known as a caring doctor who devoted his entire life to helping people in French Equatorial Africa. Yet, very few people know Albert Schweitzer as a foremost critic of biblical prophecy.

Schweitzer's book, *the Quest of Historical Jesus* triggered the first quest of eschatologial field. We call it "the consequent eschatology", or "the first quest". What was his standpoint on Christ and his teachings? This passage may shock some readers who only know Schweitzer as a doctor. Schweitzer states:

> The Jesus of Nazareth who came forward publicly as the Messiah, who preached the ethic of the Kingdom of God, who founded the Kingdom of Heaven upon earth, and died to give His work its final consecration, never had any existence. He is a figure designed by rationalism, endowed with life by liberalism, and clothed by modern theology in an historical garb.[352]

For Christians, it should be astonishing to find out that this admirable, humanitarian doctor was actually a critic of Christianity. How did he come to such a repelling conclusion? Schweizter states:

> The mistake was to suppose that Jesus could come to mean more to our time by entering into it as a man like ourselves. That is not possible. First because such a Jesus never existed. Secondly because, although historical knowledge can no doubt introduce greater clearness into an existing spiritual life, it cannot call spiritual life into existence. History can destroy the present; it can reconcile the present with the past; can even to a certain extent transport the present into the past; but to contribute to the making of the present is not given unto it.[353]

Since the 1st century, Christians throughout centuries held a firm belief that Christ would return to their generations. Schweitzer was among the first modern theologians to realize that Jesus meant to return in His generation in 1st century. He argues that although Christ intended to return in His generation, He failed to do so. From Schweitzer's point of view, the Parousia was delayed. He uses Matthew 10:23 to prove his point. What prophecy did Jesus make? Jesus was talking to his disciples when he made this prophecy.[354] "When you are persecuted in one place, flee to another. I tell you the truth, you will not finish going through the cities of Israel before the Son of Man comes."[355] Schweizter uses this time statement to prove his point:

> *He tells them in plain words (Matt. X. 23), that He does not expect to see them back in the present age. The Parousia of the Son of Man, which is logically and temporarily identical with the dawn of the Kingdom, will take place before they shall have completed a hasty journey through the cities of Israel to announce it. That the words mean this and nothing else, that they ought not to be in any way weakened down, should be sufficiently evident.[356]*
>
> *The whole history of "Christianity" down to the present day, that is to say, the real inner history of it, is based on the delay of the Parousia, the non-occurrence of the Parousia, the abandonment of eschatology, the progress and completion of the "de-eschatologising" of religion which has been connected therewith. It should be noted that the non-fulfillment of Matt. X. 23 is the first postponement of the Parousia.[357]*

Claiming the postponement of the Parousia, Schweitzer explains how the later Christians after the 1st century began to develop a belief that Christ was supposed to come on their generations:

> *The expectation of His Second Coming, repeatedly expressed by Jesus towards the close of His life, is on this hypothesis authentic; it was painted over by the primitive Christian community with the colours of its own eschatology, in consequence of the delay of the Parousia; and in view of the mission to the Gentiles a more cautious conception of the nearness of the time commended itself; nay, when Jerusalem had fallen and the "signs of the end" which had been supposed to be discovered in the horrors of the years 68 and 69 had passed without result, the return of Jesus was relegated to a distant future by the aid of the doctrine that the Gospel must first be preached to all the heathen. Thus the Parousia, which according to the Jewish-Christian eschatology belonged to the present age, was transferred to the future.[358]*

185

Every generation after Jesus' contemporaries

Schweitzer's conclusion makes it easier to understand why every generation after Jesus' generation expected the Parousia to take place within their generation. Why does every generation insist that their generation is the one that Jesus mentioned concerning the end of age?[359] The reason for this repetitive phenomenon throughout the ages is because people are so concerned about the signs that they miss the context of prophecy. Our 20th century Christian press is so concerned with signs that books that deal with the signs of the end often become bestsellers of the year, or even decade. Here's what a contemporary end time book states concerning the abundance of signs:

> *How much more reason do we have today to recognize the signs of His second coming! We are surrounded by so many obvious signs that one would have to be blind not to see them – yet some fail to recognize them even when they are called to their attention. So many signs exist today that you could write a book about them. In fact, I did, the Beginning of the End, first published in 1972 and then again in 1991. Many changes in the twenty-seven years since that book's first publication have only brought further confirmation that we are indeed living in "the times of the signs." Never in history have so many legitimate signs of Christ's return existed.[360]*

Focusing on materialistic fleshly view causes readers of the Bible to look for the literal fulfillment of prophecies. Everything that occurs around us can be interpreted as signs depending on from which perspective the event is interpreted. Therefore, interpreting various events throughout the world as signs caused us to believe that the end was imminent.

To mention only a few that might concern our immediate future, William Butler Yeats, the poet who predicted a Celtic Armageddon in 1899, seems to have expected the end of the Christian era in 2000, when the rough beast, "its hour come at last," would slouch to replace Jesus. So does the Reverend Tim LaHaye, and so did several other ecclesiastics : Protestant ministers like Robert Fleming in the eighteenth century, Robert Scott in the nineteenth century, or the Catholic canon Rodriguez Cristino Morondo in the twentieth century, Nos-

186

tradamus appears to have expected the end, or the beginning of the end, in 1999(the seventh month of 1999 to be precise), while numerological readings vary between 1999 and 2001. So apparently, does the Mayan calender. Tynetta Muhammad, a numerologist belonging to the Nation of Islam, has recalculated the code of the Koran to conclude that we may expect the end in 2001.[361]

Seeking for signs and preaching for the imminency of the end is nothing new. It has been around the world for more than two millennia. Apocalypticism, a belief that there will come an end to the sinful world, has been prevalent even before the Christianity began. Every religion has its own apocalyptic prophecy. This expectation for the end of the world somehow entered the Christian doctrine, thereby causing Christians to believe in the end time madness.

For example, the "rapture", which in some views is to remove the minority of saints from earth during the horrors of tribulation, has become part of doomsday chic. Rapture wristwatches proclaim "One hour nearer to the Lord's return." Bumper stickers re-quest "Beam me up, Lord." Dashboard signs warn, "If you hear a trumpet, grab the wheel." The *Rapture Alert Newsletter* published by Salem Kirban, *whose Guide to Survival*(1968) sold half a million copies, offers predictions of the end seasoned by recipes for Mrs.Kirban's chicken soup.[362]

In common usage, "doomsday," the day of judgment, becomes annihilation; "apocalypse" means disaster, cosmic catastrophe, the end of the world. The revelation of God's plan for the world and for his church narrows into predictors about how many times (history) and time will end; "eschatology," the doctrine of end times, becomes the chief aspect of apocalypse.[363]

Christian apocalypticism in its true sense is not apocalypticism identical to the ones prevalent in every other religion, but rather a transition from the old to new age signified by two covenants that was to take place in time of Jesus' contemporaries.

Failing to predict the exact time of the end and its significance forced Christians to repetitively emphasize the immanency of the end. Fortunately, a person lives no longer than a century in most cases. Thus this repetitive immanency remains new to many young people.

Most social historians link apocalypticism with political crisis, social change, or material distress. But this does not tell us much. Change, pain, distress, and insecurity are part of EVERY AGE; so are hope, confusion and simple curiosity.[364] The signs that Christians were supposed to look for included wars, rumors of wars, nation rising against nation and kingdom against kingdom, famines, pestilences, earthquakes, deceivers and false prophets, betrayals, hate, iniquity abounding and love waxing cold.[365]

Here's what Paul says to Timothy in his letter: "... There will be terrible times in the last days. People will be lovers of themselves, lovers of money, boastful, proud, abusive, disobedient to their parents, ungrateful, unholy, without love, unforgiving, slanderous, without self-control, brutal, not lovers of the good, treacherous, rash, conceited, lovers of pleasure rather than lovers of God – having a form of godliness but denying its power. Have nothing to do with them."[366]

If that's what we're supposed to look for, no wonder that every era produces apocalyptic visions appropriate to its circumstances.[367] Following quote shows how Eugen Weber, author of *Apocalypses*, concludes his statement concerning the repetitive end time madness: "All ages are marked by perils, lawlessness, social disorders and upheavals, breakdown of morality and family, perils, turbulence and troubles that can serve as signs and stimulate expectations. They are portents; and there are always portents, always apocalyptic apprehensions, always fears and hopes to suggest millennial themes. Joining pessimism and optimism together, the millenarian message is infinitely adaptable to the circumstances of every age."[368]

20ᵗʰ century contemporary millennialisms

The repetitive futuristic millennial views may differ in details, but they all agree on the point that Christ's Parousia remains in the future. There are three mainstreams of contemporary millennialisms: amillennialism, postmillennialism and premillennialism. Together, they belong to the futurist school of the Bible. There are many other schools such as preterists, historicists and idealists. However, the majority resides with futurism.

Most contemporary churches of our time give their followers three options to choose: amillennialism, postmillennialism, or premillennialism. The reason why there are relatively few people with opposing views is that most Christians rarely get a chance to hear about alternatives besides those three interpretations. The futuristic millennialisms can be called "the contemporary millennialisms". The followers of these three millennialisms are so numerous that other views can be ignored and still wouldn't damage the contemporary Christian doctrine.

How do these three interpretations differ from each other? I found very good definitions of these views, defined by Tim LaHaye and Jerry B. Jenkins in their book *"Are We Living in the End times"*, which is also a part of *Left Behind Series*. Note that these two scholars side with dispensational premillennialism.

Amillennialism is the belief that there is no future Millennium but that prophecy will be fulfilled in eternity. This belief crept into the church after Augustine introduced the practice of spiritualizing and allegorizing Scripture, which opened the door to many pagan doctrines and practices and helped to plunge the Western world into the Dark Age for over eleven hundred years. Times were dark because people had little access to or knowledge of the Scriptures; consequently they lost the hope of Christ's second coming.[369]

Postmillennialism is the notion that the church will evangelize this world, making it progressively better until it finally ushers in the kingdom. This belief was popularized by a seventeenth-century Anglican named Daniel Whitby. Since then it has waxed and waned in popularity according to the times. After the barbarities of World War I the doctrine suffered a sharp decline, and the catastrophe of World War II nearly finished it off. Today only a few groups still cling to the position, including those known as Reconstructionists. But the savagery of the twentieth century makes it difficult to maintain postmillennialism today.[370]

These two authors defined their two opposing views while suggesting the defects of those two. Here's how they define premillennialism: "Generally speaking, whenever people have taken the Bible at face value and interpreted it as it reads, they believe the second coming of Christ is scheduled before the Millennium unfolds; thus they are called *premillennial-ists*."[371] One remarkable feature about premillennialism, in my opinion, is that they read the Bible at face value, thus turning the biblical prophecy into a great fiction according to the read-ers' imaginations. Its example is well known today, the *Left Behind Series*. Such creative work is not possible with other views. Reading the Bible at face value – without acknowledg-ing the original recipents (1st century Christians) of the letters in the Bible – makes readers to believe that they are living in the last days. Such rule may apply well for reading novels, but we are dealing with biblical prophecies. The eschatology is not something that can be interpreted according to its readers' imaginations.

The defects of literal interpretation were dealt with already in the beginning chapters of this book. Among three futuristic interpretations, the most literal interpretation would be premillennialism, which is the most popular view among Christians in our time. It is also the most dangerous view among three, in my opinion. First, let us study how these pre-millennialists feel about their literal interpretations. Follow-ing passage is from Hal Lindsey's book, *Planet Earth: the Final Chapter*.

At the beginning of 19th century, theologians began to apply the same principles of literal interpretation to the field of prophecy that the Reformers had applied to the doctrine of Salvation. This caused a kind of "reawakening" to the reality of Bible prophecy and its growing relevance to the time in which they were living. After the close of the 1st century AD, there had developed apathy toward the study of prophecy. By the 4th century, prophecy had been writ-ten off as a collection of allegories. Such early theologians as Origin and Augustine allegorized prophecy into meaningless nonsense.[372]

What Lindsey calls the "meaningless nonsense" is directed toward spiritual interpretation of the Bible. But does he inter-pret Matthew 16:27-28, Matthew 10:23, or Matthew 24:34 literally? If anyone is interested in looking up more passages, make sure to read chapters *Prophetic Language, Great Commis-sion, Time Statements* and *Olivet Discourse*.

Lindsey has some thoughtful insights about the global trend. From his viewpoint, studying the current global event is necessary to interpret the biblical prophecy. Here are some passages from his book that gives more detail about his premillennial interpretation.

> *We believe that the Common Market and the trend toward unification of Europe may well be the beginning of the ten-nation confederacy predicted by Daniel and the Book of Revelation.[373]*
> *Heading the Revived Roman Empire will be a man of such magnetism, such power, and such influence, that he will for a time be the greatest dictator the world has ever known. He will be completely godless, diabolically evil "future fuehrer".[374]*

Above passage is what many people believe is going to happen in the future. It is true that most European nations joined the European Union and that the entire Europe looks forward to establishing a unified government. But similar events already took place several times throughout the millennia. Caesar, Napoleon and Hitler seem to be better candidates for the possiblity of the end than our concurrent events. Many people claimed the end being near even back in the days of Napoleon and Hitler, but such events never led to the end of the world.

Lindsey's books greatly amplified the premillennial interpretation over America for decades. In our decade, this premillennial movement has been even more popularized by *the Left Behind Series.*

Millennial Entertainment?

Premillennialists expect miracles and something dramatic. A good example of the millennial view according to the premillennial literal interpretation would be the *Left Behind* series that were recently published. Tim LaHaye and Jerry B. Jenkins, the authors of these books, interpreted the Bible so literally that the book *Left Behind* has become a great fiction, however, not a good interpretation of the biblical prophecy. Here are some passages from *Left Behind* concerning the prophecies from the Old Testament: *Rosenzweig's formula was fast making Israel the richest nation on earth, far more profitable than its oil-laden neighbors. Every inch of ground blossomed with flowers and grains, including produce never before conceivable in Israel. The Holy Land became an export capital, the envy of the world, with virtually zero unemployment. Everyone prospered[375].*

In order to emphasize the importance of Israel, the authors made this tiny nation of the Eastern Mediterranean into an economic giant, an economy entirely dependent on agriculture and producing flowers. Only David Ricardo would have accepted this abnormal type of economy.

There is an objection stating that Israel has been given great power historically. It is true, Jews had been given a privilege from rest of the nations, however they lost that privileged status when they rejected Jesus Christ as their Messiah and crucified him. The Jews, after rejecting Christ, needed salvation to be atoned for their iniquities. Romans 10:3 states "Since they did not know the righteousness that comes from God and sought to establish their own, they did not submit to God's righteousness."

Israel and Jerusalem play significant roles in dispensational premillennialism – the perspective taken by *Left Behind* authors. It is true that there are many prophecies concerning Israel and Jerusalem that have to do with the end of age. The dillema that dispensationals face in this case would be that both the literal Israel and temple are gone. They have to bring back the 1st century elements, which only existed in the 1st century. Without the temple or the city of Jerusalem fortified by literal walls, there can be no fulfillment of prophecies concerning the end of age.

As he approached to Jerusalem and saw the city, he wept over it and said, "If you, even you, had only known on this day what would bring you peace – but now it is hidden from your eyes. The days will come upon you when your enemies will build an embankment against you and encircle you and hem you in on every side. They will dash you to the ground, you and the children within your walls. They will not leave one stone on another, because you did not recognize the time of God's coming to you."[376]

"When you see Jerusalem being surrounded by armies, you will know that its desolation is near. Then let those who are in Judea flee to the mountains, let those in the city get out, and let those in the country not enter the city. For this is the time of punishment in fulfillment of all that has been written."[377]

Above were the prophecies concerning the fall of Jerusalem. Note that the fall of Jerusalem is included as a part of

Great Tribulation, which is mentioned in Luke 21, Matthew 24 and Mark 13.

Another prophecy where they have to rebuild the temple is in 2 Thessalonians. Paul wrote to the church of Thessalonica: "Don't let anyone deceive you in any way, for that day will not come until the rebellion occurs and the man of lawlessness is revealed, the man doomed to destruction. He will oppose and will exalt himself over everything that is called god or is worshiped, so that he sets himself up in God's temple, proclaiming himself to be God."[378]

From the dispensational perspective, this cannot be fulfilled until the temple of Jerusalem is rebuilt. Hence, they strive to rebuild or reconstruct in our time the elements that only existed back in the 1st century.

Rebuilding of the Temple?

The Second Temple was destroyed back in 70 AD. To replace the old literal temple, Christ gave us a heavenly temple through his crucifixion. Paul wrote to Ephesians concerning this heavenly temple.

Consequently, you are no longer foreigners and aliens, but fellow citizens with God's people and members of God's household, built on the foundation of the apostles and prophets, with Christ Jesus himself as the chief cornerstone. In him the whole building is joined together and rises to become a holy temple in the Lord. And in him you too are being built together to become a dwelling in which God lives by his Spirit.[379]

Then, why do premillennialists insist on rebuilding the old temple of Jerusalem that have nothing to do with our salvation? What does LaHaye and Jenkins say about this issue? Following passage is excerpted from their book, *Are We Living in the End Times?*

All prophecy teachers who interpret the Scriptures literally agree that the Jewish temple in Israel will be rebuilt.
The first temple, built by Solomon, was destroyed by the Babylonians in 586 B.C. The second temple – begun in 535 B.C. and completed in 516 B.C., then lavishly renovated by Herod the Great starting in 19 B.C. – was destroyed by the Romans in A.D.

70. That there will be a third temple is predicted by the prophet Daniel, the apostles Paul and John, and none other than the Lord Jesus Himself. They all taught that Israel's third temple will be rebuilt either before the Tribulation begins or soon thereafter, for it is seen in copmlete operation by the middle of the Tribulation, when it will be desecrated.[380]

The logic behind this argument is quite simple. Neither Jesus nor the apostles ever mentioned of the temple being REBUILT. They mentioned about the temple, of course, but that doesn't necessarily mean that the temple mentioned in the prophecy is the third temple. Bible never mentions about the third literal temple. LaHaye and Jenkins conclude their passage by following statement.

Obviously, since Israel does not now have a temple, the third temple must be rebuilt for such an event to occur.[381]

Without rebuilding the literal temple, we know for certain that from the dispensational premillennial perspective, the Parousia is never going to take place. This point is emphasized again in that book by those two authors.

Israel's temple plays an important role in several end-time prophecies of the Tribulation. The Antichrist is going to desecrate that temple halfway through the Tribulation – but to do so, it must first be rebuilt.[382]

Acknowledging the fact that all the Middle Eastern conflict revolves around that Jewish temple site, one should realize how serious the end time madness has become. It is not something we could simply laugh about. Rebuilding the Jewish temple could actually trigger another World War! Premillennialism is not a mere interpretation of the Bible, but it has become a movement toward the future global conflict. For such reason, I say that premillennialism is the most dangerous view that Christian could take among three futuristic millennial views. Unfortunately, it is also the most popularized view in the media.

Our media tends to be more sympathetic toward the Jewish situation than toward Palestinians'. Palestinians in TV are often viewed as extreme terrorists who believe in Holy

War paradigm, while the Jews are seen as the victims of those so-called terrorists. But in reality, Palestinians are the ones who are being suppressed, not the Jews. The conflict started, because Jews and Christians attempted to rebuild the Jewish temple. However, it first necessitates destroying the mosque. The mosque that stands on the old temple site is one of three sacred mosques of Islam. Premillennial movement encourages rebuilding the temple, thereby ignoring the religious rights of Muslims and Palestinians who live there.

In order to secure their status in Jerusalem, Jews force Palestinians to move out of the city. Among them are Palestinian Christians who are being told to move, because many contemporary Christians believe that God has granted Israel privilege over Gentiles. Although we already know that the manifestation of spiritual Israel has made the literal Israel of no significance, people with contemporary eschatology still believe that Jews are still God's people who are superior to the ones saved in Christ. What has our church become? Everybody is equal in Christ; the Jews do not have any special privilege over anybody. If Christ does not make any difference, then why don't we just all convert to Judaism?

The position taken by premillennialists sympathizes with the Jewish cause while suppressing the Palestinian Christians. Lindsey comments: "Weeks before the war, Arab families were encouraged to abandon their homes and flee to the Arab countries. They were assured that within a matter of weeks, they would be allowed to return and reclaim their homes – and also the homes of the massacred Jews. Although the new Israeli government pleaded with them to stay and fight together for a common homeland, all but a handful crossed over into Jordan to wait for total victory against the Jews. They expected to return home as soon as the hated Jews were slaughtered. Instead, after the war was lost, their "brother" hosts kept them in miserable refugee camps and did nothing to help them."[383]

What is the consequence of rebuilding the temple, besides the next World War? Will Christians be able to attain anything from the rebuilt temple? It could be a tourist attraction, obviously. However, that has nothing to do with our salvation. From the contemporary millennial perspective, rebuilding the temple is crucial, because the literal temple does not exist anymore. In order to fit their map, they have to rebuild a temple for the end to come, the end which has already come in 70 AD.

The end was to come in the 1st century, as the previous chapters concerning the Parousia explained. That is what the apostles and 1st century Christians believed, too. Now we, the 20th century Christians, have to re-create the 1st century aspects in our 20th century world to make our world fit for last days setting. What is the consequence of contemporary millennialisms? To which direction does the misinterpretation of the Bible lead us?

⌘

6.3. Transforming Future Church

Beginning with the 1st century church established by Christ Himself, many churches thrived in their ages. However, among all the churches that flourished in the past, not a single one continues to have as much influence as they did in the past. We know for a fact, that 1st century church is nonexistent in our time. Eastern Orthodox had been active back in the last days of Roman Empire and throughout the early Middle Age, but after the fall of Constantinople in 1453 the religion lost its influence over Mediterranean and has become more local than global.

Catholic church is an excellent example of such trend, in which a church married to an age is a widow in the next.[384] After its separation from the Eastern Orthodox, the church has influenced the Western Europe for nearly 1,500 years. However, after confronting the Protestant Reformation, it has become relatively weaker than it used to be.

A church married to an age is a widow in the next. This single phrase describes all the churches that existed from Christ's time to our time. It may still apply to the churches that exist in the present era and beyond. Why are churches doomed to decline? The doctrinal, theological challenges from outside of the church, makes the church obsolete. The church that grows old and obsolete is doomed to fade away.

Back in the 1st century, the old covenant Jews had to face the challenge from Christians, the challenge that they considered "heretical". The old covenant started to fade away after the new one came, as Paul said "By calling this covenant "new", he has made the first one obsolete; and what is obsolete and aging will soon disappear."[385]

The issue of misinterpretation and faults within the doctrine causes the collapse of a church. It is not some matter that can be ignored or be put in consideration in the future time. In order for the 20th century church to avoid being a widow in the upcoming era, it is crucial that we look back at our doctrine and see what error we might have.

In our post-modern era, Christianity has lost more influence as other religions expanded rapidly. For example, Islam has become the second-largest religion in the world, and it is now the fastest growing religion on earth. In North America there are now over 4 million Muslims. Some researchers claim that there are now more Muslims than Jews in North America, which would make Islam the second-largest religion in the United States and Canada.[386]

Muslims are not the only critics of Christianity. Many other religions, cults and atheists criticize the errors within the Christian doctrine. Unfortunately, very few contemporary Christians have knowledge on their own doctrine to support the uniformity of Bible.

At this rate, the entire Christian church – not individual denominations but all the church, could become a widow in the next era. What is the necessary change that we have to make in order to create a safe world for Christianity? It is the contemporary Christian doctrine that we should be able to fix and reconstruct. The Christian doctrine in this sense is the interpretation of the Bible, not the Bible itself. Bible itself is perfect, I'm not asking to change the words in the Bible. Changes are needed in our interpretation of the Bible, the way which we read and understand the Bible.

Many Christians tend to be emotional about the church, but they neglect the true understanding of the Bible and Christian doctrine. It is such grace that we have an opportunity to understand how we obtain our relationship with God. Theology should not be restricted to the elders, preachers or theologians, but it should be studied thoroughly among all Christians who are eager to learn the message that God gives us through the Bible. If we can make this happen, then we are making a big difference in our world. Transforming Christian emotion into true faith and understanding is the only way to prevent our Christian church from becoming a widow in the next era. "A church married to an age is a widow in the next." It is about time this phrase becomes history. Let's work together to make an exception, to build a different world.

⌘

6.4. Contemporary Dilemma

Many faithful Christians in this world have a hope; they hope that Jesus would come in clouds and lift the believers up in the air to meet Him. The earth will be destroyed, and then the life that they have led to that point will be meaningless. They will live in a paradise and there will be no sorrow, tear, war, etc.

This is the supposed resolution of contemporary eschatology. They wait for the time of the end when everything will change. This future hope is the motivation that led Christians throughout the centuries to live on in this weary world. They relied on this hope; that in a distant future there will come a day when every Christian can throw away all the responsibilities that they were obligated to. "Jesus come quickly and get me out of this mess!" This is the future hope that all Christians have been told to hold for two millennia from the time of Christ.

Some claim that the past fulfillment of Parousia robs us of hope that we have held for two thousand years. But is this hope what we were supposed to hold in the first place? What if this hope had been already fulfilled? Paul wrote a letter to the church of Thessalonica around AD 50. He wrote:

According to the Lord's own word, we tell you that we who are still alive, who are left till the coming of the Lord, will certainly not precede those who have fallen asleep. For the Lord himself will come down from heaven, with a loud command, with the voice of the archangel and with the trumpet call of God, and the dead in Christ will rise first. After that, we who are still alive and are left will be caught up together with them in the clouds to meet the Lord in the air. And so we will be with the Lord forever. Therefore encourage each other with these words.[387]

The letter was addressed to the Christians in Thessalonica who were waiting for the Lord's return. They were about to witness the greatest moment of history when they will be caught up to be in God's presence. We are living in 20th century, nearly 1,900 years after the fulfillment of Parousia. We do not realize, but we are living in God's presence. We have a direct relationship with God through Jesus Christ. God is with us; God is omnipresent.

Then, what is the point of this so-called future hope that we long for so desperately? This hope, in other words, is a mere desire for an escape from reality. Although we have our relationship with God through Christ's blood, we are not satisfied with this type of spiritual fulfillment of hope. Throughout millennia, what we had been longing for was a salvation in physical sense, a hope that we'd be able to throw away all the responsibilities and worries that we have to deal with in this world; such as job, school, home, etc. Many Christians wait for the earth to be burned up so that they would not have to work anymore, or to deal with non-Christians. They maintain their pessimistic view on this world; however, many hesitate to make a single attempt to make a difference.

We should realize that this worldly pessimism is a consequence of contemporary eschatology. Instead of searching for a way to make a better world, we search for another world. We wait for the earth to be burned up so that we won't have to deal with all the problems associated within this world. Such worldly pessimism is what our Christianity had been all about. No wonder we Christians have been rejected by others so bitterly.

This chapter will deal with the consequences of contemporary eschatology. There are two consequences in broad sense besides the worldly pessimism. A person who denies Christ as his Savior can either denounce his entire belief on deity or he can choose other religious doctrines that suit him best. Before getting into detail about these two consequences, we have to understand why a person would want to reject Christ as his Savior.

The limit of inspirational evangelism

The Christian evangelism has grown rapidly in this century through media. Evangelists search every possible way to preach the gospel, and in our century they preach in TV, radio and even on the Internet.

One day, I watched a sermon from one Christian channel. I was amazed to see the preachers in TV being very enthusiastic. They had the eloquence to touch the people's heart and to draw them near God. They turned on some soft music to create an inspirational atmosphere within the building. I believe that there were several thousand people listening to the preacher.

It should be an encouraging sign to us Christians that there are many evangelists working through media. The media is what is going to determine the outcome of Christian evangelism in the 21st century. We should thank God for granting us such an effective tool to preach the gospel.

These inspirational programs are designed to touch people's heart and to renew their faith. They are the flickering lights that light a candle called "faith". Unfortunately, these programs are literally "flickering lights"; the majority of people who are touched by these programs do not maintain their spiritual walk in Christ. They may strive to be more Christian for a short period of time, but they return to their old ways of living after a while. This is the limit of inspirational evangelism.

Obviously, these programs do not get into much detail concerning theology. Rather, they pick verses and use them for moral and inspirational purposes. They rarely suggest any eschatological significance within the Bible. Emotion based faith may be powerful for a short period of time, but they eventually fade away.

Russell's challenge

The contemporary Christian faith, which lacks proper theology, stands weak against growing atheism and agnosticism. There are many skeptics of the Bible; these skeptics usually argue that God cannot be proven scientifically. That is one of their main arguments, and there are some atheists who use the Bible to find itself contradictory. For most cases, they attack the contemporary Christian eschatology.

Bertrand Russell, a self-claimed atheist suggested the defects within Christ's teaching in his essay "Why I am not a Christian". He found Christ's eschatological teaching contradictory to the contemporary Christian doctrine.

201

For one thing, He certainly thought that His second coming would occur in clouds of glory before the death of all the people who were living at that time. There are a great many texts that prove that. He says, for instance, "Ye shall not have gone over the cities of Israel till the Son of Man be come."[388] Then he says, "There are some standing here which shall not taste death till the Son of Man comes into His kingdom"[389]; and there are a lot of places where it is quite clear that He believed that His second coming would happen during the lifetime of many then living. That was the belief of His earlier followers, and it was the basis of a good deal of His moral teaching.[390]

He reasons that since Christ failed to fulfill what he said that he would, Christ is a failed apocalyptic prophet.

He thought that the second coming was going to be very soon, and that all ordinary mundane affairs did not count. I have, as a matter of fact, known some Christians who did believe that the second coming was imminent. I knew a parson who frightened his congregation terribly by telling them that the second coming was very imminent indeed, but they were much consoled when they found that he was planting trees in his garden. The early Christians did really believe it, and they did abstain from such things as planting trees in their gardens, because they did accept from Christ the belief that the second coming was imminent. In that respect, clearly He was not so wise as some other people have been, and He was certainly not superlatively wise.[391]

How does the contemporary eschatology respond to that argument? The premillennial literalists, while striving to interpret all the verses literally interpret the time statements symbolically. Why do they have to contradict their literalist policy? Yet, none of them gives any answer to Matthew 10:23. In order to fit the biblical prophecy into their perspective, they have to distort the time statements and create the 1st century setting in our 20th century. These theological weaknesses allow Russell and other atheists to criticize Christianity and other religions.

Religion prevents our children from having a rational education; religion prevents us from removing the fundamental causes of war; religion prevents us from teaching the ethic of scientific co-

operation in place of the old fierce doctrines of sin and punishment.
It is possible that mankind is on the threshold of a golden age; but,
if so, it will be necessary first to slay the dragon that guards the
door, and this dragon is religion.[392]

In other words, Russell is saying that God – or the concept of deity – must be purged from humanity if one hopes
for the future progress. The contemporary Christian theology,
which could not properly counter non-Christians' arguments
concerning the end time prophecy, couldn't provide a good
reason for people to have faith in the Bible. Many dissatisfied
Christians simply walk away their churches, saying, "The Bible
contradicts itself."

The traditional Puritan life centered on the Bible is no
longer visible in the present day America. Christians had best
face the fact that the Bible-centered values are no longer "main-
stream" to the American way of life. Everybody lives in a
cultural context of godlessness and anti-Christian philosophy.
Nowhere is this quite so apparent as in the sphere of sexual
ethics.[393]

Growing cults' and other religious doctrines

Many cults and other religions claim that they have solu-
tions to the modern world's relative moral decline, however,
in all cases they are unbiblical. While cults preach against the
social problems and expand every single second, all that contemporary Christians discuss about is simply how to expand
their members as opposed to the cults, not dealing with the
genuine problem – the false end time teaching.

Christians losing their faith on the Bible is a serious
problem to be dealt with. One of the worst consequences that
can happen to a Christian is to lose his or her faith. Lack of
faith deters them from studying the words of God, the Bible.
After they walk out their churches, these ex-Christians realize
that they cannot live without the spiritual comfort that they
once received by being in the church. At the end, they search
for different religious doctrines and pick one that suits them
best.

There are many religious movements preying upon
Christians. Among them are Muslims, Jehovah's witnesses,
Mormons, New Age, Buddhism, Scientology, Christian Sci-

ence, Baha'i, etc. Probably besides Buddhism which started 500 years before the time of Christ, all these religious movements deviate from the Bible claiming that the Bible is corrupted, or that it is not written by the divine inspiration called "the Holy Spirit." Some of them write their own Bible.

How do other religious doctrines deviate from the Bible? Let's examine, in this case about Islam faith. Robert Morey has encountered many Muslim arguments. Following are the passages from his book "the Islamic Invasion".

In countless encounters with Muslims, whenever the Quran contradicts some particular verse in the Bible, they have always said, "The Bible is corrupted at this point."

When I ask for some kind of proof that the Hebrew or Greek text is corrupt, they respond by saying, "I do not have to prove it is corrupt. It has to be corrupt, otherwise it would agree with the holy Quran."

For example, the Quran contradicts the Bible in that it denies that Jesus was crucified.[394]

If the Christians of the past centuries realized the fact that the Parousia had been fulfilled in AD 70, and that both the vision and prophecy was sealed up[395], then there wouldn't have been any confusions such as other religious doctrines. The majority of other religious doctrines were created after Christ's time. They are the results of past centuries' eschatology.

The Future Hope?

Many people I've encountered claim that the past fulfillment of Parousia robs the future hope of Christianity. Someone even said, "I'm not going to let Jesus get away without fulfilling the hope." He meant it literally.

If this hope of Second Coming was not the one that we were supposed to look for, that if this hope had been already fulfilled, then what hope do we have as Christians? Max R. King tells us what we have now.

What does all of this mean to the believer, and especially to us today? First, it means that all the saints who have departed this life over the past 2,000 years are not still waiting for the benefits of Christ's second coming. But because Christ has already come at *a time and in a manner that fully consummated God's redemptive purposes, the perfection and eternal reward of past saints were secured in physical death. As citizens of an eternal kingdom, such is our hope today. But if Christ's coming to us **while we are living on earth** is our hope of Christ, then millions have died without ever having had it. On the other hand, if the primary purpose of Christ's coming was for the benefit of a system rather than for the individuals living at that time, then it is advantageous to all to have his second coming closely connected with his first coming. This means that the benefits of his second advent are now fairly and impartially dispensed to all saints of all ages through the system perfected by his second coming. Therefore, all share alike in the blessings of his second advent, and physical death does not create a gap or waiting period, as would be true if his coming and its results were still future.[396]*

We should realize what we have as Christians. Some people ask, "What comes after AD 70?" There should be a future hope that would guide us through the third millennium. This "future hope" should be able to transform our world so that it is proper to be called "the new covenant world".

> *This is the covenant I will make with the house of Israel*
> *after that time, declares the Lord.*
> *I will put my laws in their minds*
> *and write them on their hearts.*
> *I will be their God,*
> *and they will be my people.*
> *No longer will a man teach his neighbor,*
> *or a man his brother, saying, 'Know the Lord,'*
> *Because they will all know men,*
> *from the least of them to the greatest.*
> *For I will forgive their wickedness*
> *and will remember their sins no more.[397]*

We have a hope for the better future; our new covenant faith must be spread throughout the world to put an end to the conflicts caused by many different millennial views. How should our church be transformed in order to achieve better future? The future lies in our hands. What can we do to bring a new future?

⌘

6.5. Rebuilding a Foundation for Christianity

Jay Gary once stated in his lecture, *the Mystery of History*, during the seminar over Atlanta last February that "evangelicalism thrives on distinction, engagement, conflict, and threat." He also mentioned that in Christian evangelism, "God at War" paradigms ruled tradition and history. It is true that a considerable number of Christian evangelists unintentionally threat people by preaching the false eschatology. Such a method of evangelizing may be effective in short term, but arousing fear out of people's heart is not the true way to preach Jesus and his kingdom.

Disregarding the danger of false end time teachings, the present churches simply concentrate their efforts on increasing the church members. Fortunately, there are some Christians who are willing to study the Bible with open minds. However, the majority of Christians remain to be highly skeptical. They insist on their peculiar millennial views even if they are unbiblical. Max R. King mentions this issue in his book, *the Spirit of Prophecy*.

"But in spite of this long history of human error, some are so egotistical as to refuse any admission of error within themselves. Some would rather attribute error to the thinking and writing of the apostles than to admit the error is within the framework of their own thinking. This may be due in part to the fact that some segments of Christian evangelism have placed such emphasis upon possessing the truth that they have defeated their own purpose, in that they have made some so fearful of not having all of the truth that they are afraid to study the Bible with an open, searching mind. If they were to do this, they might discover new truth and feel guilty and condemned for having once been without it. Consequently, a closed mind, crystallized traditions, and a "head in the sand" philosophy have thwarted growth in grace and knowledge."[398]

The truth vs. tradition

The beginning section of this book mentioned about Luther's refusal to submit to the traditional Catholic teachings. What strengthened Luther to stand against the popes and councils, who had a thousand years tradition behind it? It was *the truth* that enabled him to go through all the hardships from the persecutions. Recall what the emperor Charles V said; "A SINGLE FRIAR WHO GOES COUNTER TO ALL CHRISTIANITY FOR A THOUSAND YEARS MUST BE WRONG."[399] But ask yourself this question, "Who sided with the truth? The 16th century Catholic priests, or Martin Luther and the Protestants?" It seems as if this new idea does not stand a chance against the millennial views with two thousand years tradition behind them, however, only the truth reigns supreme at last.

Another parallel can be found in the first century church. Right after Christ's crucifixion and until the siege of Jerusalem, it seemed as if Christianity was going to end up being a mere sect of Judaism. However, everything changed after the destruction of the temple of Jerusalem in AD 70. Between those two events, many enthusiastic Christians such as Paul preached against the Jewish traditional view of the Scripture. Christians were greatly outnumbered, but now Christians are outnumbering the Jews by hundreds of millions of followers.

A building with weak foundation cannot last long

Charlie Stewart, Josh's dad, once made a statement concerning the contemporary Christianity; "A building with weak foundation cannot last long." This is very true. Many churches in general put a heavy emphasis on evangelism. However, they simply ignore clarifying the theological issues. They are so concerned with their expansion, yet they do not realize that they have weak theological foundations. Such houses cannot last long. The reason why there are so many denominations comes from purely theological issues. Christianity has remained divided since its beginning, the Jewish ministry and the Gentile ministry. There are countless many denominations that few Christians know exactly how many Christian denominations there are and even fewer Christians memorize the names of all the denominations.

This is simply my opinion, but I believe it is necessary that Christians put their priority on reforming the Christian doctrine first and then emphasizing its dissemination afterwards. A building with weak foundation cannot last long. What we do as students of the Word is to emphasize the significance of theology in the church, thereby building a strong foundation. The end time teaching has been the cause of controversies for nearly two millennia. Solving this problem is related with almost all the social issues that we encounter with today.

Until the authority of the Bible is recognized by men, the reestablishment of morality in our world will remain only a dream. Until prophetic preaching is heard by people in the pews, there will be no reversal of present trends to even grosser immorality. Until people who claim to believe and to follow the Bible demonstrate their profession through rigorous separation from the things of the world, "righteousness" will remain merely an archaic word in the contemporary vocabulary.[400]

⌘

Epilogue: Reforming the Church Through Eschatology

Changing the course of history is not a simple task. It cannot be achieved in an instant moment. Such a movement requires time, effort and perseverance. Without these elements, there cannot be any movement.

For two thousand years, Christians have been told to wait and hold fast for the Second Coming. Now we know that the Parousia took place back in AD 70, we have a new task at hands. The task is to change our perspective on theology. Theology has been neglected among the average Christian individuals since the beginning of early church; the church elders and preachers – fearing the possible controversies and divisions among the church members - have encouraged us to do so. If we believe in the future coming, we may as well ignore it saying, "It's going to pan out at the end." However, we can't just sit back anymore knowing that the Parousia took place in AD 70.

Christian faith cannot survive unless the Christian emotion and theological understanding unite together. Understanding how the Bible works actually enhances our spiritual walk in Christ. The truth is a motivation for courage that cannot be suppressed with any type of force.

The neo-reformation should start with an emphasis upon the significance of understanding theology. Understanding the Bible helps us in our relationship with Christ more than anything does, it sets a flame on our faith and strengthens it.

There is a major difference between true faith and blind faith. The blind faith simply draws a person away from reality, while the true faith helps a person to gain courage, strength and confidence. Faith should be a personal conviction and understanding of truth through constant, diligent study.[401] This faith is what a new covenant man needs to live in God's presence. Many Christians wait to be caught up in God's presence. They

211

do not realize that they are LIVING in God's presence. This is a simple message that we preach to others. Understanding this simple phrase is all we need to transform our church to thrive in the third millennium and ages to come.

We must reform the church through eschatology. By preaching the uniformity of biblical eschatology, we are putting an end to the denominational conflicts and many other social consequences resulting from the contemporary eschatology. We should realize that we are all under one building, the holy temple of the Lord. Finally, we should transform our Christian church to be a lampstand for the Third Millennium. With a single phrase "We are LIVING in God's presence", we are changing the course of history, and the future of this world. Will you be one of us?

⌘⌘

Prologue: Luther's Refusal

1 Eph. 2:22
2 I have no intention of criticizing the 20th century Catholic church. The Catholic church reformed itself through the Counter-Reformation movement, as opposed to the Reformation movement of the Protestants.
3 William J. Duiker and Jackson J. Spielvogel, World History, vol.I (Belmont, California: Wadsworth Publishing Company, 1998ed.), 534
4 Ibid., 534

Introduction: truth vs. tradition

5 Mark 7:8
6 Matthew 23:30
7 Ephesians 2:21

Part 1: Essentials in Christian Eschatology

1.2. Enslaved to the Physical Realm

8 Romans 8:5-7
9 Romans 6:18-20
10 Romans 6:1-6
11 1 Peter 1:4
12 1 Corinthians 15:44b
13 Hebrews 10:1a

1.3. The Context of Scripture

14 2 Timothy 3:16

1.4. Prophetic Language

15 2 Peter 1:19-21
16 Isaiah 13:6-10
17 It does not mean that I agree with the commentator.
18 Matthew 24:29
19 Matthew 24:30
20 1 Corinthians 15:51-53
21 1 Thessalonians 4:15-17
22 Numbers 10:1-10
23 Leviticus 16:2
24 Arthur Melanson, The Second Coming Postponed or Fulfilled? (Audubon, New Jersey: Joy of the Lord, 1998ed.), 28

1.5 Seeking the Spiritual Quest

25 Hebrews 10:10
26 visit www.skepticsannotatedbible.com
27 Max R. King, Old Testament Israel and New Testament Salvation (Eschatology Publications: Warren, Ohio), 1
28 Luke 11:9-10

Part 2: Covenantal Perspective

2.1. Problems with the Law

29 καταργουμενον, the present tense, meaning: is being annulled rather than past tense was. Some other commentators translated so that it would fit with their perspective of the Old Covenant ending at the crucifixion of Christ in AD 33 rather than at the Fall of Jerusalem in AD 70.
30 Hebrews 10:16
31 James 1:15
32 1 Corinthians 15:56
33 1 Corinthians 15:53-54
34 Romans 8:2; Hebrews 9:15
35 Romans 3:19

36 Romans 2:12
37 Revelation 20:11-15

2.2. Resolution to Sin

38 Romans 8:1-4
39 Romans 6:14-15
40 Jeremiah 31:31-34
41 Isaiah 42:6; Isaiah 49:6
42 1 John 3:9
43 Romans 4:14-15
44 1 John 1:8
45 Daniel 9:24

2.3. The Story of Abraham

46 Genesis 15:1-6
47 Genesis 16:1-4
48 Genesis 16:4-6
49 Genesis 16:15-16
50 Flavius Josephus, Antiq. 1.10.4.
51 Genesis 17:1-8
52 Genesis 17:9-11
53 I will plant Israel in their own land, never again to be
uprooted from the land I have given them.
54 John 10:27-28
55 Hebrews 12:28, Ephesians 3:21
56 Romans 4:13
57 Max R. King, the Spirit of Prophecy (Warren, Ohio: Park-
man Road Church of Christ, 1983ed.), 26
58 Genesis 17:15-18
59 Genesis 17:19-21
60 Flavius Josephus, Antiq. 1.12.4.
61 Genesis 18:1-2
62 Genesis 18:8

63 Genesis 18:9-15
64 Flavius Josephus, Antiq. 1.12.2.
65 Flavius Josephus, Antiq. 1.12.3.
66 Flavius Josephus, Antiq. 1.12.3.
67 Genesis 21:8-14

2.4. Transfer of the Covenants

68 Romans 5:13-14
69 Luke 22:20
70 Galatians 4:21-23
71 Galatians 4:24-25
72 Galatians 4:26-28
73 Isaiah 26:1
74 Galatians 4:29-31
75 Luke 21:12; 16-17
76 Romans 5:12-14
77 1 Corinthians 15:45

Part 3: First Century Christianity and Judaism

3.1. Two Audiences of Ministry

78 Acts 10:44-48
79 Acts 10:9-23
80 Acts 11:1-3
81 Acts 11:4-17
82 Acts 11:18
83 Acts 15:7-11
84 Acts 20:22-23
85 Acts 21:10-12
86 Acts 21:13-14
87 Acts 21:26
88 Acts 21:24
89 Galatians 3:10-14

90 Galatians 4:30
91 Hebrews 8:13
92 Galatians 3:1-5
93 Acts 15:1

3.2. Great Commission

94 Jay Gary, The Star of 2000 (Colorado Springs, Colorado: Bimillennial Press, 1994ed.), 40

3.3. Holy Spirit and the Last Days

95 Joel 2:28-32
96 Acts 2:16-17
97 1 Corinthians 1:5
98 1 Corinthians 1:7
99 1 Peter 1:4-5
100 Ephesians 1:13-14
101 Mark 16:15-18

3.4 Historical Atonement

102 1 Corinthians 15:56
103 Romans 7:7-11
104 Hebrews 9:1-5
105 JESUS and His Times (Pleasantville, New York: the Reader's Digest Association, Inc., 1987ed.), 138-140
106 Leviticus 16:15-17
107 Hebrews 9:6-10

Part 4: The Fall of Jerusalem

4.1. Martyr of Stephen

108 Acts 6:8

109 Acts 7:48-53
110 1 Thessalonians 2:14-16
111 Matthew 23:29-36
112 Max R. King, the Spirit of Prophecy (Warren, Ohio: Warren Printing, Inc. 1983ed.), 33

4.2. Causes of the Rebellion

113 Mark 2:15
114 Flavius Josephus, War 2.10.4
115 War 2.14.1
116 War 2.14.2
117 War 2.8.6
118 JESUS and His Times (Pleasantville, New York: the Reader's Digest Association, Inc., 1987ed.), 217
119 Ibid., 217

4.3. Unexplainable & Unquestionable Signs

120 Flavius Josephus, War 6.5.3
121 War 6.5.3
122 War 6.5.3
123 Tacitus, Histories 5.13
124 Flavius Josephus, War 6.5.3
125 Tacitus, Annals 15.38
126 Annals 15.44

4.4. Jewish War

127 Flavius Josephus, War 2.17.2
128 War 2.17.8
129 War 2.17.9
130 War 3.1.3
131 War 3.1.3
132 War 3.4.1

133 War 3.7.23

134 War 3.7.36

135 War 5.1.1

136 War 5.1.4

137 War 5.1.3

138 War 5.1.3

139 Luke 21:20-22

140 Tacitus, Histories 5.1

141 Histories 5.12

142 Flavius Josephus, War 5.10.2

143 War 5.10.3

144 War 5.6.1

145 War 5.6.1

146 War 4.3.10

147 War 4.3.13

148 Matthew 24:15

149 Flavius Josephus, War 5.10.4

150 War 5.10.5

151 War 5.6.3

152 Flavius Josephus, Trans. William Whiston, the Works of Josephus: Complete and Unabridged (Peabody, Massachusetts: Hendrickson Publishers, Inc., 1987ed.), 710

153 War 5.11.1

154 War 5.12.3

155 Matthew 24:21

156 Flavius Josephus, War 5.13.4

157 War 5.13.6

158 War 6.4.3

159 War 6.4.5

160 Flavius Josephus, Trans. William Whiston, the Works of Josephus: Complete and Unabridged, 743

161 War 6.6.1

162 War 6.9.1

163 Flavius Josephus, Trans. William Whiston, the Works of Josephus: Complete and Unabridged, 749

164 War 6.9.4
4.5. Arrival of Apocalypse
165 Will Durant, Caesar and Christ (New York: Simon and Schuster, Inc. 1944ed.), 547
166 Ibid., 545
167 Ibid., 549

Part 5: the Arrival of Christ

5.1. The Olivet Discourse

168 Matthew 24:1-3
169 Mark 13:4
170 Matthew 24:14
171 Matthew 24:15-18
172 Matthew 24:21
173 Daniel 12:1-2
174 Luke 17:20-21
175 Matthew 16:28
176 Zechariah 9:13-14
177 Matthew 24:34
178 Tim King, Jack C. Scott, Jr., Covenant Eschatology: A Comprehensive Overview (Warren, Ohio: Living Presence Ministries, 1998ed.), 20
179 Matthew 24:36
180 Matthew 24:38-41
181 2 Peter 3:9
182 Matthew 24:40-41
183 Matthew 24:13
184 Luke 17:34-37
185 2 Peter 1:20-21

5.2. On Revelation of Jesus Christ

186 Philip Yancey and Tim Stafford, The Student Bible, New

International Version® (Grand Rapids, Michigan: Zondervan Publishing House, 1996ed.), 1316
187 Hebrews 9:8
188 Hebrews 9:24
189 Hebrews 9:28
190 Luke 21:27-28
191 Revelation 1:19-20
192 Revelation 2:14-16
193 Revelation 3:11-13
194 Revelation 10:9-11
195 Gene Fadeley, Revelation: Kingdoms in Conflict (Charlotte, North Carolina: Anchor Publishing, 1995ed.), 33
196 Ibid., 33
197 Revelation 14:6-7
198 Don K. Preston, Who is this Babylon? (no publisher listed, 1999ed.), 158
199 Daniel 8:17
200 Daniel 8:26
201 Revelation 5:3-5
202 Daniel 12:8-9
203 Revelation 22:10
204 The Olivet Discourse is recorded throughout Matthew 24, Mark 13, Luke 21, Luke 17, etc.
205 Hebrews 9:28

5.3. Covenants in Revelation

206 Galatians 4:29
207 Gene Fadeley, Revelation: Kingdoms in Conflict (Charlotte, North Carolina: Anchor Publishing, 1995ed.), 35
208 Ibid., 35
209 Revelation 11:7-10
210 2 Corinthians 3:7
211 Galatians 3:10
212 Zechariah 5:1-4

213 John 14:2-3

214 Hebrews 10:1

215 Above quote was taken from NRSV Bible, because NIV changed every sentence of that chapter to past tense from the original Greek text.

216 Revelation 15:5-8

217 The following passage is also a reference that signifies God's judgment over the old covenant, but this chapter is more focused looking at Revelation from the covenantal perspective.

218 Leviticus 26:14-19

219 Revelation 13:15-18

220 Kenneth C. Davis, Don't Know Much About the Bible (New York: William Morrow and Company, Inc. 1998ed.), 464

221 Max R. King, the Spirit of Prophecy (Warren, Ohio: Warren Printing, Inc. 1983ed.), 318

222 Ibid., 318

223 Galatians 4:29-30

224 Revelation 14:15-16

225 Matthew 24:40-41, 1 Thessalonians 4:17

226 Matthew 24:30, Revelation 1:7

227 Revelation 14:18-20

228 Matthew 23:29-37, 1 Thessalonians 2:13-16

229 Matthew 13:24-30

230 Matthew 21:33-40

231 Galatians 4:30

232 Matthew 21:41

233 Matthew 21:43-44

234 Matthew 21:45

235 Revelation 20:4-6

236 Gene Fadely, Revelation: Kingdoms in Conflict, 73

237 Revelation 20:3, 5, 7

238 2 Corinthians 3:7

239 Gene Fadely, Revelation: Kingdoms in Conflict, 74

240 Ezekiel 37:11-14
241 Revelation 20:13-15
242 Romans 6:16
243 Romans 4:14-15
244 1 Corinthians 15:56
245 Revelation 21:1
246 Matthew 5:18 (NRSV)
247 Matthew 5:18
248 Matthew 24:35
249 Hebrews 12:26-27
250 Isaiah 24:19
251 Isaiah 51:16
252 Revelation 21:3-4
253 Ephesians 2:21-22
254 Hebrews 12:22
255 Revelation 21:22
256 Revelation 21:11-14
257 Revelation 21:18-21
258 Flavius Josephus, War 5.5.7
259 Revelation 1:6; Revelation 20:6

5.4. Judgment in Revelation

260 Joseph Campbell, the Hero with a Thousand Faces (Princeton, New Jersey: Princeton University Press, 1968ed.), 374
261 Isaiah 63:2-4
262 Olivet Discourse (Matthew 24; Mark 13; Luke 21)
263 Luke 21:22
264 Luke 21:28
265 Leviticus 26:14-16
266 Leviticus 26:40-42
267 Isaiah 51:17-20
268 Isaiah 51:21-23
269 Luke 19:41-44
270 Ezekiel 7:1-3

271 Ezekiel 7:10-11
272 Ezekiel 7:13-14
273 Ezekiel 7:15-16
274 Ezekiel 7:22
275 Ezekiel 7:25-27
276 For further study, look at Matthew 23
277 Leviticus 26:18
278 Leviticus 26:21
279 Leviticus 26:23-25
280 Leviticus 26:27-30
281 Hosea 10:8
282 Luke 23:26-31
283 Revelation 6:15-17
284 Luke 21:23
285 Revelation 12:9
286 Revelation 13:1-2
287 Daniel 7:7
288 Daniel 7:14
289 Revelation 21:1
290 Revelation 13:18
291 Revelation 17:4-6
292 Zechariah 5:5-8
293 Acts 17:1-9
294 1 Thessalonians 2:13-16
295 Matthew 23:32
296 Matthew 23:34-36
297 Revelation 18:4-5
298 Revelation 18:24
299 Don K. Preston, Who is this Babylon? (no publisher listed, 1999ed.), 157-158
300 Revelation 20:7
301 Matthew 22:1-3
302 Matthew 22:4
303 Matthew 22:5-7
304 Matthew 22:8-10

305 Matthew 22:11-12
306 Matthew 22:13-14
307 Revelation 20:11-15
308 Romans 2:12
309 Hebrews 8:12
310 2 Corinthians 3:7
311 1 Corinthians 15:53-56
312 Romans 4:14-15
313 Matthew 27:25
314 Gene Fadeley, Revelation: Kingdoms in Conflict (Charlotte, North Carolina: Anchor Publishing, 1995ed.), 49-50

5.5. Atonement in Revelation

315 Jim McGuiggan, the Book of Revelation (St.Lubbock, Texas: Montex Publishing Company, 1978ed.), 16
316 Hebrews 9:28
317 Revelation 1:13
318 Gene Fadeley, Revelation: Kingdoms in Conflict (Charlotte, North Carolina: Anchor Publishing, 1995ed.), 15
319 Revelation 4:10
320 1 Chronicles 25
321 Gene Fadeley, Revelation: Kingdoms in Conflict, 16
322 Revelation 4:4
323 Leviticus 8:6-9
324 1 Peter 2:9; Revelation 1:6; 5:10
325 1 Chronicles 24:5
326 Max R. King, the Spirit of Prophecy (Warren, Ohio: Warren Printing Inc., 1983ed.), 282-283
327 Revelation 7:14
328 Revelation 1:6
329 Revelation 8:2-5
330 Leviticus 16:11-14
331 Leviticus 16:18-19
332 1 Thessalonians 4:16

333 1 Corinthians 15:52

334 Note that this passage is commonly used to dismiss the possibility of past fulfillment.

335 Revelation 1:7

336 Robert DiYanni, LITERATURE: Reading Fiction, Poetry, Drama, and the Essay (The McGraw-Hill Companies, Inc., 1998ed.), 1898-1899

337 Isaiah 40:3-5

338 Robert DiYanni, LITERATURE: Reading Fiction, Poetry, Drama, and the Essay, 1920

339 Matthew 26:64

340 Luke 21:31

341 Luke 17:20-21

342 Revelation 1:7

343 Leviticus 16:17

344 Hebrews 9:8; please use the Greek-English Interlinear, or NRSV if permissible, since translations are usually biased due to the translators' perspectives. It is best to use the Greek-English Interlinear, which is the original text of the New Testament.

345 Hebrews 9:28

346 Revelation 21:3-4

347 2 Corinthians 3:7

348 Revelation 21:6-7

Part 6: Neo-Reformation

6.1. Historical Reformation

349 Mark 7:9 (NRSV)

350 Matthew 10:23, Matthew 16:27-28, Matthew 24:34, Mark 13:30, Luke 21:32

6.2. Classical and Contemporary Millennialism

351 Gary Holloway, the College Press NIV Commentary James & Jude (Joplin, Missouri: College Press Publishing Company, 1996ed.), 119-120
352 Albert Schweitzer, the Quest of Historical Jesus (Baltimore, Maryland: The Johns Hopkins University Press, 1998ed.), 398
353 Ibid., 399
354 Matthew 10:1-5
355 Matthew 10:23
356 Albert Schweitzer, the Quest of Historical Jesus, 358-359
357 Ibid., 360
358 Ibid., 233
359 Matthew 24:3
360 Tim LaHaye, Jerry B. Jenkins, Are We Living in the End Times? (Wheaton, Illinois: Tyndale House Publishers, Inc., 1999ed.), 26-27
361 Eugen Weber, Apocalypses (Cambridge, Massachusetts: Harvard University Press, 1999ed.), 28
362 Ibid., 28-29
363 Ibid., 29
364 Ibid., 31
365 Ibid., 31
366 2 Timonthy 3:1-5
367 Eugen Weber, Apocalypses, 28
368 Ibid., 33
369 Tim LaHaye, Jerry B. Jenkins, Are We Living in the End Times, 237-238
370 Ibid., 238
371 Ibid., 238
372 Hal Lindsey, Planet Earth: the Final Chapter (Berverly Hills, California: Western Front Ltd., 1998ed.), 30
373 Hal Lindsey, the Great Works of Hal Lindsey (New York: Inspirational Press, 1994ed.), 76

374 Ibid., 78
375 Tim LaHaye, Jerry B. Jenkins, Left Behind (Wheaton, Illinois: Tyndale House Publishers, Inc., 1995ed.), 8
376 Luke 19:41-43
377 Luke 21:20-22
378 2 Thessalonians 2:3-4
379 Ephesians 2:19-22
380 Tim LaHaye, Jerry B. Jenkins, Are We Living in the End Times, 121-122
381 Ibid., 122
382 Ibid., 128-129
383 Hal Lindsey, Planet Earth: the Final Chapter, 71

6.3. Transforming Future Church

384 I heard that phrase first used by Jay Gary in his lecture, Mystery of History, back at Atlanta seminar on February 25th, 2000. Contact LPM@livingpresence.org for further information.
385 Hebrews 8:13
386 Robert Morey, the Islamic Invasion (Eugene, Oregon: Harvest House Publishers, 1992ed.), 6

6.4. Contemporary Dilemma

387 1 Thessalonians 4:11
388 Matthew 10:23
389 Matthew 16:28
390 Bertrand Russell, Why I am not a Christian (New York: Simon & Schuster, Inc. 1957ed.), 16
391 Ibid., 16-17
392 Ibid., 47
393 Rubel Shelly, Going on to Maturity (Nashville, Tennessee: 20th Century Christian, 1983ed.), 55-56
394 Robert Morey, the Islamic Invasion (Eugene, Oregon:

Harvest House Publishers, 1992ed.), 6
395 Daniel 9:24
396 Max R. King, the Spirit of Prophecy (Warren, Ohio:
Warren Printing Inc., 1983ed.), 262-263
397 Hebrews 8:10-12

6.5. Rebuilding a Foundation for Christianity

398 Max R. King, the Spirit of Prophecy (Warren, Ohio:
Warren Printing Inc., 1983ed.), 113
399 William J. Duiker and Jackson J. Spielvogel, World History, vol.I (Belmont, California: Wadsworth Publishing Company, 1998ed.), 534
400 Rubel Shelly, Going on to Maturity (Nashville, Tennessee: 20th Century Christian, 1983ed.), 60

Epilogue: Reforming the church through eschatology

401 Max R. King, Old Testament Israel and New Testament
Salvation (Warren, Ohio: Eschatology Publications, 1990ed.), 1